ANDY WARHOL

First published in the United States of America in 1997
by UNIVERSE PUBLISHING
A Division of Rizzoli International Publications, Inc.
300 Park Avenue South
New York, NY 10010

and THE VENDOME PRESS

ISBN 0-7893-0086-9

Printed and bound in Italy

Library of Congress Catalog Card Number: 97-060139

UNIVERSE OF ART

ANDY WARHOL

By Philippe Trétiack

UNIVERSE / VENDOME

driving around in a Rolls, owning a château, an island, diamonds, winning a gold medal or the Nobel Prize is wonderful – in fact, it's more than that, but to have been painted by Andy Warhol is better, much better, perhaps even the best. Warhol is the only artist to have succeeded, in the most profane fashion, in turning anyone into an icon of modern times – the most contemporary sacred act. After this, however much artists tried to invent as many *mises en scène* and happenings as they liked, they still remained within the bounds of what he had accomplished – there will always be a pre- and a post-Warhol and that post-Warhol period is having difficulty establishing itself.

Warhol confused the issue – he sabotaged modern art through parodies, commercial reprocessing and divergences on all fronts. He placed the electric chair and Marilyn Monroe on the same level, and popularized the image of an America in all its most relentlessly commercial aspects – worse than that, he popularized everything and even made a style of it: Pop art. In those vital years of triumphant 'isms', when Pollock and de Kooning's Abstract Expressionism reigned supreme over the great art of painting, heir to Cubism, Fauvism and other forms of Pointillism hatched in Europe, Warhol broke free. But the concept of 'Popism' has never caught on. Warhol was not the sort to allow himself to be cornered.

For Warhol was, above all, a runaway – a refugee, from war and from poverty. His family had emigrated from a Slovak village in the Carpatho-Rusyn mountains, settling in Pittsburgh – city of steelworks, hell on earth. There Andrew Warhola, Andy Warhol as he became known, was born on 6 August 1928. He was to maintain an artistic haze around his date of birth – was it 1929 or 1933? Warhol grasped the century's growing obsession with 'youthfulness' and so decided never to reveal his age again. In 1949 he fled from the provinces and set off for New York with his mother. She was a secretive figure, central to his apotheosis, *pasionaria* of a son beatified in his own lifetime, it was she who usually kept watch in the shadows of the 'factory'. At this stage, Warhol showed above all a talent for drawing. He adopted a technique consisting of blotted lines – going over a pencil drawing in ink and applying it, while still wet, to another sheet of paper. The randomness of the result conveyed all the ambiguity the artist was to cultivate between the original work and the copy. While most artists besieged the art galleries, he tackled the pages of the magazines and got his first job at *Glamour* magazine. Contributing to fashion magazines, creating 'ads', the beginning of Warhol's career was founded on compromise. He sold his art and would never cease to do so, and even made his own style of it. Within ten years, he became one of the greatest illustrators of shoes in New York – he was acknowledged as the Leonardo da Vinci of footwear.

Artists provided themselves with studios, and Warhol set himself up in a space which he called the 'factory'. He was the product of pure capitalism and of the blast furnaces – he was a machine, reprocessing anything he laid his hands on. For Warhol the reclamation of mass-produced painting was the summation of it all. He was a master at manipulating, distorting, turning things upside down – silkscreen prints, reproductions, fake posters, rip-offs, in all of these he proved Marcel Duchamp's point: everything can be art. Warhol went even further and sensed the dawning of an age in which the artist would become the finest part of his work. So he set himself at centre stage and created the Pop attitude – wigs, leather and decibels. He became the image of his own sacrifice, aware that he would have to change continuously, become a professional dissident.

Throughout the fifties, Warhol worked fast and, among other things, published picture books at his own expense. He invested in a wardrobe with an inclination towards the ragged chic – he would drip paint on his exquisite Brooks Brothers shoes and wear ties that reached down to his knees. He transformed his apartment into a glory-hole, living in an atmosphere of 'Victorian Surrealism'. He earned lots of money and figured in a list entitled *1000 Names and Where to Drop Them*, under the heading 'big business'.

On 16 June 1952, the first Warhol exhibition opened in New York, consisting of fifteen discreet drawings illustrating the stories of Truman Capote. The critics saw in them affinities with Cocteau, Balthus and Toulouse-Lautrec. There was an element of American folk art in his line and this appealed to the public. In 1956, his popularity increased when some of his images of footwear were selected for the exhibition 'Recent Drawings USA' held at the Museum of Modern Art in New York.

Three years later, Warhol understood it all. He shifted from illustrated pages to painting and chose as a theme the pages of magazines. Like Rauschenberg and his outline of the coca-cola bottle, he played with differences in scale. He began to paint comic strips, sensing that vulgar art would lead him to an art that was more noble. Warhol possessed exceptional powers of intuition – New York was already in revolt; artists were fed up with abstraction and they turned to 'scavenging', routing around in waste bins. Consumer society was under pressure – hijacking, plunder and theft, anything was permitted to artists. While Rauschenberg turned this into a speciality by, for example, asking de Kooning for a drawing and, with large sweeps of the rubber, transforming it into a Rauschenberg, Jasper Johns reprocessed the American flag. Nevertheless, alongside the Johns and Rauschenbergs exhibited at the Castelli Gallery, Warhol still cut a poor figure. Any fame he enjoyed was founded on his commercial work, which was not evolving.

By 1961, the scene was definitely changing – photography posed a threat to illustration and Warhol began to lose commissions so he decided to advertise alone. He produced his first portrayals of the Campbell's soup can – this reinterpretation of the still life marked the advent of consumer goods as subject matter for the artist and an image of society as a whole, but at the same time it conferred on these products a morbid, very Caravaggesque metallic appearance. The cans sent shivers down the spine, the supermarket display became art gallery pastiche. The European press saw it as a Marxist criticism of capitalism, but it certainly wasn't. Blessed with ubiquity, Warhol did not take a stand – like his soup cans, he was unaware of any hidden depth. In 1962 Claes Oldenburg exhibited in the window of his 'shop' all sorts of foodstuffs, overturning the barriers between the artist's atelier, the exhibition space and the market place. In February, Roy Lichtenstein exhibited paintings and comic strips at the Castelli Gallery. Warhol realized that he could no longer show his own comic strips without being accused of plagiarism. The Pop artists, the plunderers of their time, had absolutely no desire to be accused of plundering from each other. Warhol therefore concentrated on form and devoted himself to serial composition, the draughtboard, and in his search for powerful symbols, he opted for the most powerful of all: the dollar. In 1962, like a forger, he took up silkscreen printing.

Warhol appeared in *Time* magazine in the midst of an article devoted to the Pop art movement. With a totally vacant mind, a vocabulary limited to 'terrific', 'fantastic' and 'wow', he created for himself the role of provocateur without opinions. When receiving potential buyers, he would bore them to death by playing the same record over and over again – repetition was his weapon, as was directness. Entirely lacking in finesse, Warhol went straight to the point. He drew anything famous – the faces of American starlets, the brand names of biscuits and since the press was in the limelight he also took an interest in the 'news'. On 4 June, he hijacked the 'front page' of the *New York Mirror* and produced *129 Die in Jet*, the first appearance of the macabre in an oeuvre that was never to break free from it. Because Warhol's intuition was perfect he sensed that violence, atrocities and the electric chair were going to become symbols of America just as Judy Garland and hamburgers were. He knew that everyone would soon be discussing the burning issues of a nation imitated in all its successes and failures by the entire western world. The reaction was hostile – Warhol was accused of stealing his subject matter and, worse still, of screen printing it. All the same, he had hit lucky – after *129 Die in Jet*, he moved on to *210 Coca-Cola Bottles*. Warhol was to write 'buying is much more American than thinking', so was making money.

On 5 August, the death of Marilyn Monroe shook the whole of America. With his necrophagous instinct, Warhol acquired a photograph taken in the fifties and screen printed hundreds of images of the actress's face. At the end of the year, he exhibited at the Sidney Janis Gallery in New York – although it was the mecca of Abstract Expressionism it was still an achievement. Warhol benefited from the interest that had by then been aroused by artists acknowledged before him. Together, they represented a popular urban trend known as the 'New Realists', 'Neo-Dadaists', 'Vulgarists', 'Commonists' and 'Factualists'. *The New Yorker* described their collective show as 'an exhibition that has hit the art world with the force of an earthquake'. Pop art had erupted onto the scene.

The consecration of Pop art occurred on 13 December 1962 when a symposium was organized at the Museum of Modern Art. From then on, nothing, whether architecture, fashion, or homecrafts was to escape the tidal wave. The following year every museum in the country attempted to put on its own show of Pop art. Warhol plunged into the macabre, with among other works, *Suicide, Saturday Disaster* and *White Car Crash*. In his hypnotic repetition of shock subjects, he exposed and contributed to the establishment of one of the motivating forces of our century: repetition breeds familiarity and then boredom. Warhol realized that the mangled remains of cars and human bodies had become elements of the American scene and of modernity itself. On impulse, Warhol embarked on a series of Liz Taylor, of Elvis with pistol in hand, of huge guns, of Marlon Brando sporting Hell's Angel gear and, subsequently, of race riots. In mixing celebrities and various phenomena, he became the eulogist of all that global information was soon to become: a hotchpotch of races and blood.

In 1963, Warhol turned to the film camera. He was to make numerous films – long, aggressive and homosexual in nature. Warhol's dream was to become a leader of the underground avant-garde, even though he denied it: 'How could I be "underground", since I've always wanted to be noticed?' Warhol turned himself into the subject of his own *mise en scène*.

At the end of 1963 Warhol moved to a loft at 231 East 47th Street. Visitors christened it the 'factory' since paintings were mass produced there. A cult spot that became a part of New York legend, the 'factory' became the epicentre of Pop culture – parties, amphetamines, scandals, encounters. Warhol's films were dreadful, but projected onto the wall of a room, like a vulgar, moving wallpaper, they improved on acquaintance. Warhol, who already went around with a Polaroid, acquired a tape-recorder – he thought any moment could become one of pure artistic creation. He collected objects and moments in time.

In 1964, Warhol pulled off a great coup, exhibiting cardboard grocery boxes at the Stable Gallery. These were wooden replicas of the cardboard 'Brillo' boxes. As he piled them up, the controversy exploded – for there was more to meditate upon in Warhol's works than to see. Writing in *Arts Magazine*, Sidney Tillim described Warhol's act as 'a gesture of aggressive passivity'. The exhibition aroused considerable interest but, in financial terms, it was a fiasco. That same year, the impact of American art definitively made its mark on the world and signalled the decline of Abstract Expressionism – for the first time, the major prize at the Venice Biennale was awarded to an American: Rauschenberg. The eyes of the world turned to New York. In 1965, in the wake of the furore, caused by the grocery boxes, Warhol was finally invited to exhibit at the Castelli Gallery, along with Lichtenstein and Rosenquist – the three greatest exponents of Pop art.

That autumn, the reputation of the already ill-famed 'factory' was tainted further. A neighbour, Dorothy Polder, fired a shot into the building, piercing several works. Warhol did not even bother to repair the canvases, which became the *Shot Through Marilyns* – reprocessing as ever. On 27 October, Fred Herko, a regular visitor to the 'factory', committed suicide by throwing himself from one of its windows. Warhol dedicated a painting of white flowers to him. They had been exhibited at the Castelli Gallery, where they were interpreted by malevolent critics as pansies, hence as a reference to homosexuality. The *Flowers* series completely deconstructed any notion of topology since it was impossible to tell whether one was looking at an aerial view of the flowers or at an elevation. Warhol churned his paintings out as though on an assembly line, producing at his peak, with the aid of friends who happened to be passing by, twenty-four in a single day. The number of flower paintings made at the 'factory' is estimated at nine hundred.

Warhol continued his career as a film maker using underground stars. Enthusiastic praise gave way to caustic comment. In 1964, *The Village Voice* published a letter from the independent film maker P. E. Goldman: 'I have tolerated praise of films shot without cameras, films shot without lenses, films shot without film, films shot out of focus but the ... praise of Andy Warhol was a bit too much.'

Warhol was ahead of the times and recognized before anyone else the kitsch and sensual power of transvestites and drag queens like Mario Montez. His films were soon graced by performers with outlandish names: Ingrid Superstar, Ultra Violet, Candy Darling, Holly Woodlawn. When Warhol appeared at the opening of the exhibition 'Three Centuries of American Painting' at the Metropolitan Museum of Art, the crowd showed more interest in his yellow glasses and in the mauve tights and pyjamas of his companion Edie Sedgwick than in the works on show. Warhol's response was: 'we were not at the the show, we were the show'. Everywhere, Andy and Edie played on their androgynous resemblance which, twenty years later, was to be all the rage.

In spring 1965, 'The 50 Most Beautiful People' party was organized at the 'factory'. Judy Garland, Rudolf Nureyev, Tennessee Williams, Montgomery Clift all stepped out of the lift in turn and Warhol savoured his triumph. He knew they belonged to the past and that from now on the world would have to reckon with the stars of his own Pop galaxy.

In order to increase his credibility, Warhol was forced to take preventive measures in his 'factory'. Notices were put up forbidding the use of drugs, but the *habitués* continued to plunge syringes into their veins quite openly. Warhol turned a blind eye. By now, however, he caused a mini-riot wherever he went – cornered in a university building, the ceiling had to be hacked down so he could escape by scrambling over the roof. At a party held at the 'factory', Roy Lichtenstein and his wife turned up disguised as Warhol and Edie, faces powdered and continuously repeating the word 'fantastic'. Warhol the plunderer began to be plundered.

Warhol was always searching for more and switched his attentions to music. Although he had never extolled the use of hallucinogens, he opened a psychedelic nightclub where the distortions of sound and light mimicked the effects of a dose of LSD. He discovered the Velvet Underground and their leader, Lou Reed, and introduced them to the singer Nico, who joined the group, reinforcing the charisma that was lacking in this wilfully mediocre and amateurish group. The band toured the country and in New York a psychiatrists' conference was forced to adjourn because of their noise. Warhol became the artist who had made the 'shrinks' flee. The group established themselves in a nightclub called the Dom, which became an off-shoot of the 'factory'. During the same period, Warhol had a second exhibition at the Castelli Gallery, showing his helium-filled balloons resembling clouds, which were related to Claes Oldenburg's soft sculptures. The whole troupe then left for California. The group, now rechristened Exploding Plastic Inevitable, played at the party to celebrate the opening of his show at the Ferus Gallery, attended by Dennis Hopper, Jim Morrison and Sonny and Cher. In the rock 'n' roll atmosphere of 1966, Warhol designed the celebrated banana record sleeve for the Velvet Underground and Nico. But these escapades also had their downside – Warhol was not among the artists selected to represent America at the Venice Biennale, the reason being that many people found his group of cranks extremely disturbing. And, in fact, like a whirlwind, Warhol no longer went anywhere unless accompanied by a sizable escort.

The 'factory' spread to nightclubs and also to the Chelsea Hotel, which became an obligatory transit point for everyone who was anyone in Pop circles. It was there that Warhol filmed *Chelsea Girls*, a sinister view of America in the sixties, deemed pornographic it was banned in Boston. *Time* magazine christened Warhol the 'Cecil B. DeSade' of the underground cinema. The film's success meant Warhol had to acknowledge that, in terms of fame, he was well on the way to outdoing everybody else. He embarked on a series of self-portraits, but nihilistic as always, although conscious of the worth of his image, he immediately devalued it, transforming it into a consumer product of the times. He continued to consider himself as a plaything for the rich. His plaything was Ultra Violet, a girl who seemed to possess the inborn talent of always being in the right spot to be caught by photographers' cameras. She proved to be the perfect escort for Warhol, who was increasingly exposed and increasingly explosive.

In 1967, at Expo '67 in Montreal, in the splendid pavilion designed by Buckminster Fuller, Warhol's own features were exhibited over an area of more than twenty square metres, next to such giants as Barnett Newman, Robert Motherwell, Frank Stella and Jasper Johns. At the end of the following year, Warhol, who usually expressed himself in a series of 'ums' and 'supers', embarked upon a career as a university lecturer. Rapidly tiring of this, he decided to send one of his friends in disguise in his place – Warhol thus pushed his concept of art to its extreme. This time, the forger was no longer deceiving the public about his work but about the artist. When the hoax was uncovered by a wily student, Warhol was elevated to the status of supreme master of mystification.

On 3 June 1968, Warhol arrived late at the new 'factory' situated at 33 Union Square, between East 16th and East 17th Street. Valerie Solanas, an old acquaintance, and the founder and sole member of SCUM (Society for Cutting Up Men), was waiting for him. She stepped out from the lift and fired her gun. Warhol was hit by two bullets and rushed to hospital in a critical condition. Six years after exhibiting his plane crashes, symbols of the disorder of modern times, he was to exhibit the effects of crime in the form of his very own flesh. The editor of *Life* magazine was not far wrong when he accused him of having breathed a hint of madness into American society. Warhol had played so much on confusion that many even suspected him of having staged his attempted assassination. Warhol was no longer the same – paranoid, he would tremble when the lift stopped at his floor. He nurtured his scars and began to display them, a follower of a brutal body art and harbinger of the piercing that was to become so popular. Richard Avedon took a huge and macabre close-up photograph. At the end of the year, he published the 400-page 'tape novel' entitled A, which *Time* described simply as 'Zzzzzzzz'. Warhol was losing his edge.

Warhol's close shave with death pushed him towards a heightened sensuality. He painted buttocks and penises. This was also the era of *Oh, Calcutta!* and *Hair*. Anyone entering the 'factory' had to lower their trousers so that Warhol could photograph their genitals with his Polaroid. He experimented voraciously and made several attempts to employ air and wind in an effort to adhere to the Land Art movement which was fast expanding at the time. In 1969, he embarked on a new challenge, setting up *Interview* magazine – having parodied the press, he now submitted himself to it.

In 1970, the number of Warhol exhibitions was continuing to increase, and the whole world was fighting over his representations of an America of which he had become the greatest propagandist, *Big Torn Campbell's Soup*, painted in 1962, was sold in New York for $60,000. On 1 May 1971, the Whitney Museum of American Art organized a Warhol retrospective and the artist displayed his work against a background of wallpaper depicting cows' heads. He revealed his talent as a punchy window dresser, but was mechanical, vulgar and aggressive – a personification of America. Omnipresent in New York, Warhol became friendly with Mick Jagger, who commissioned him to design the record sleeve for the *Sticky Fingers* album, resulting in the famous zip. When President Nixon returned from China, at the height of the period of ping-pong diplomacy, Warhol began his *Mao* series. He had never before gone so far in simultaneously criticising politics and reprocessing by devaluing all points of reference. In subsequently choosing to paint Nixon in order to champion the candidature of his challenger McGovern, 'because

Nixon is the better known of the two', Warhol proved that he was, first and foremost, the greatest artistic director of the post-war era.

While the 'factory' moved yet again, Warhol transformed himself into portraitist to the famous. Yves Saint Laurent, Golda Meir, David Hockney, Muhammad Ali, politicians, artists, athletes all ended up on his canvas. Warhol slipped from bohemian New York into the international jet-set. In *The Philosophy of Andy Warhol (From A to B and Back Again)*, as much in self-defence as to aggravate resentment, he wrote: 'Making money is art and working is art and good business is the best art.' Warhol thought that rather than buy an expensive painting, you should hang the money on the wall, so that it would be the first thing people saw when they came in the door. Warhol seemed to be noting the death of art. Nevertheless, he did several experiments with paintings oxidized with urine; then he produced his *Shadows* series and the *Reversed Marilyns* series, disturbing negatives of his own works. In this self-consumption, Warhol was already post-modern rather than modern. In 1984, the 'factory' moved once more, this time to a building owned by Warhol himself – he was becoming respectable. He accumulated thousands of objects in locked rooms and in drawers fitted with false bottoms filled to bursting with watches and jewelry. He collaborated unsuccessfully with Basquiat and eventually turned to commercial art again, accepting commissions. Warhol's signature had become a commodity in its own right. He subsequently appeared in the television series *Love Boat* and produced a cable TV programme which was to remain famous: *Andy Warhol's Fifteen Minutes*. As a result of so many skin treatments and collagen injections, his face no longer had anything natural about it – he was becoming exhausted. On 21 February 1987, he was rushed to hospital, dying there later that night, alone. He was fifty-nine. Once the shock and the grief had died down, exaggerated rumours began to circulate, the artist became a myth – perhaps Andy Warhol was not really dead and his body was simply another fake, this explosive artist's final act.

With hindsight, it is easier to grasp that in the exhilaration of his colours, his cow wallpapers, his flowers, his Marilyns and his Maos, Warhol was inviting us to watch art's *grand finale*. Post-Warhol there is a great silence, a darkness and a universal disenchantment – in a certain sense, Warhol, an explosive mixture of cunning and naïvety, even killed modern art. 'Once you thought Pop, you could never see America the same way again', he said. Plagiarizing him and thus rendering him the greatest homage of all, we could also add that post-Warhol it is the world itself and Warhol especially that we can never see the same way again.

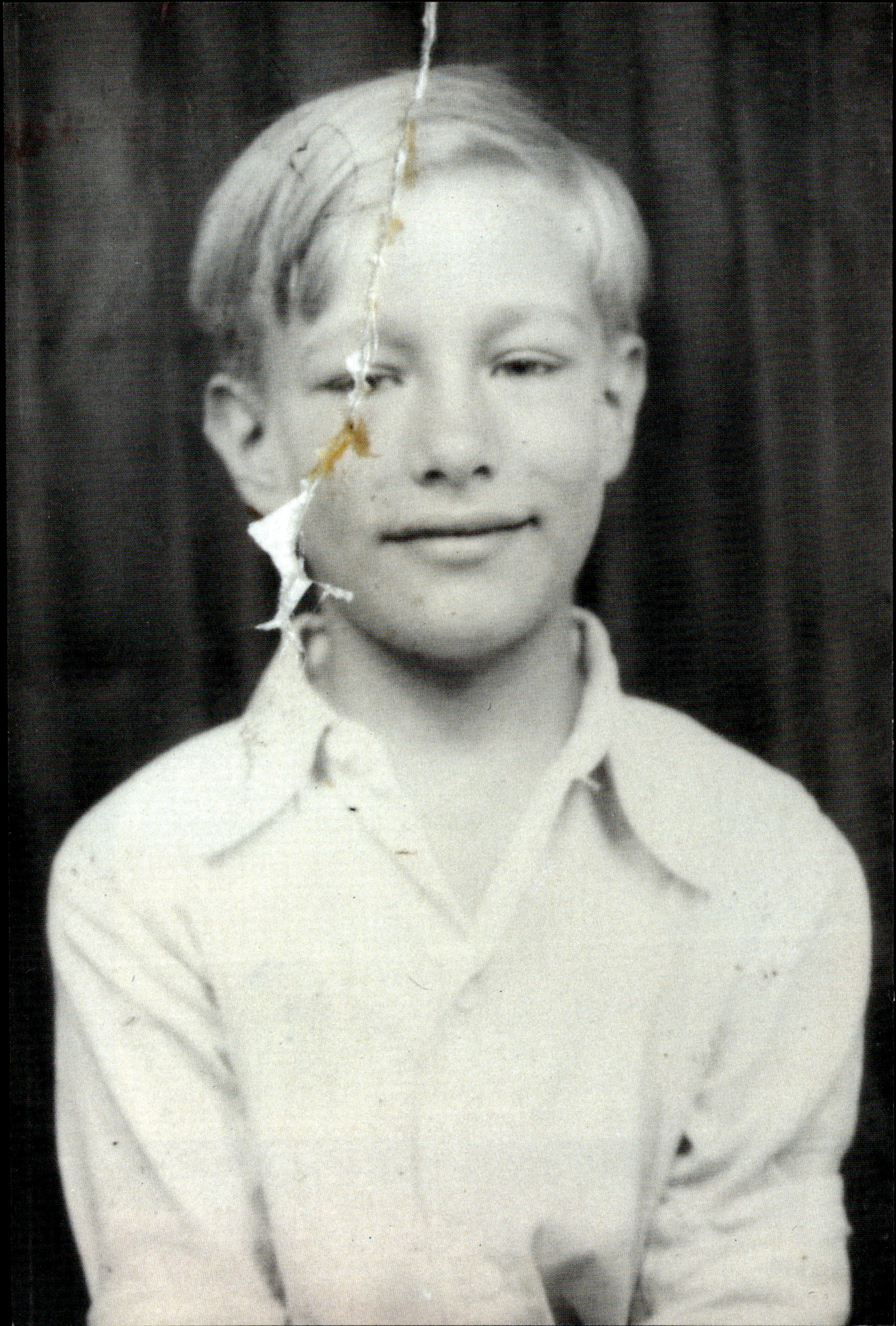

US
AIR MAIL
7¢

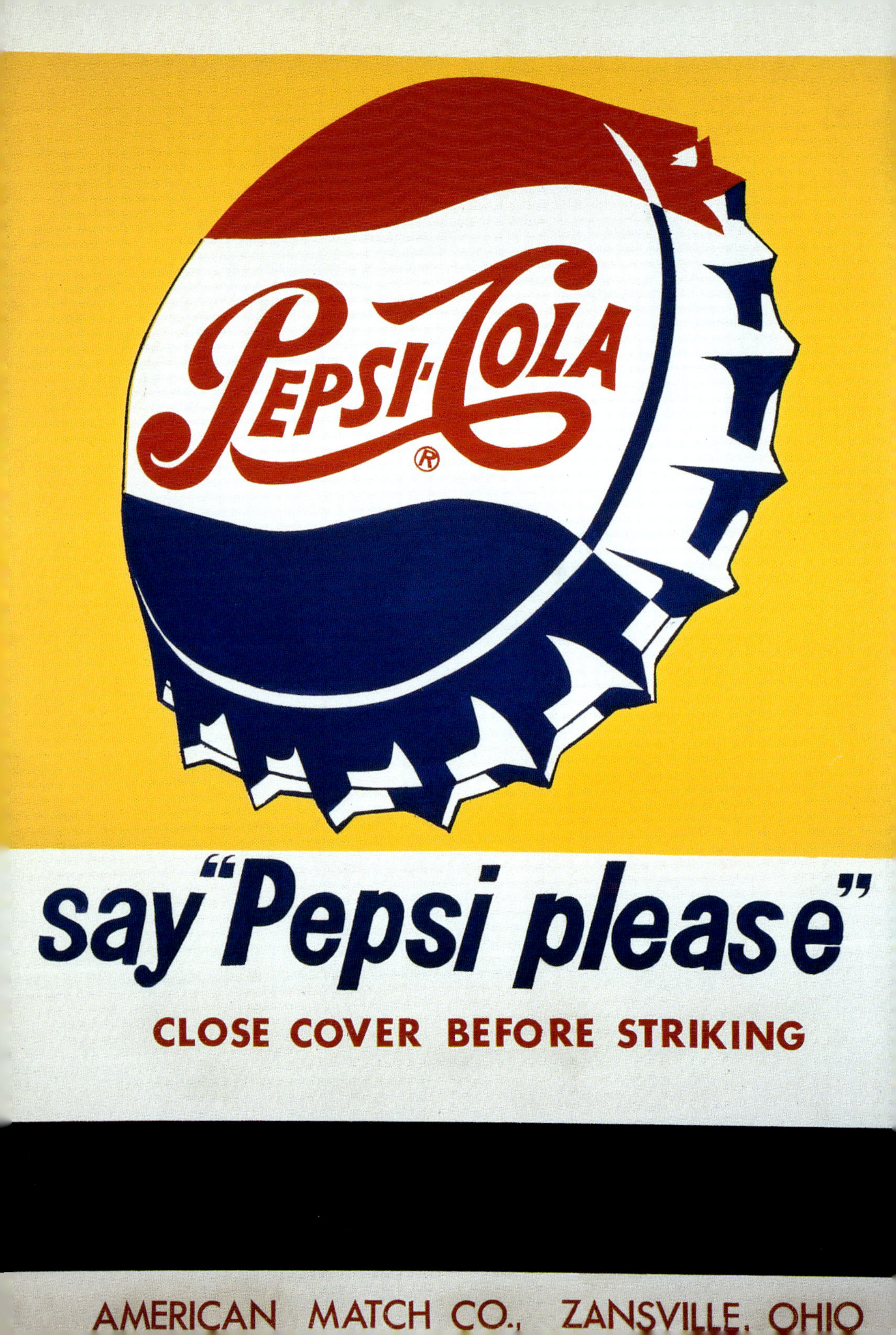
Pepsi-Cola
say "Pepsi please"
CLOSE COVER BEFORE STRIKING
AMERICAN MATCH CO., ZANSVILLE, OHIO

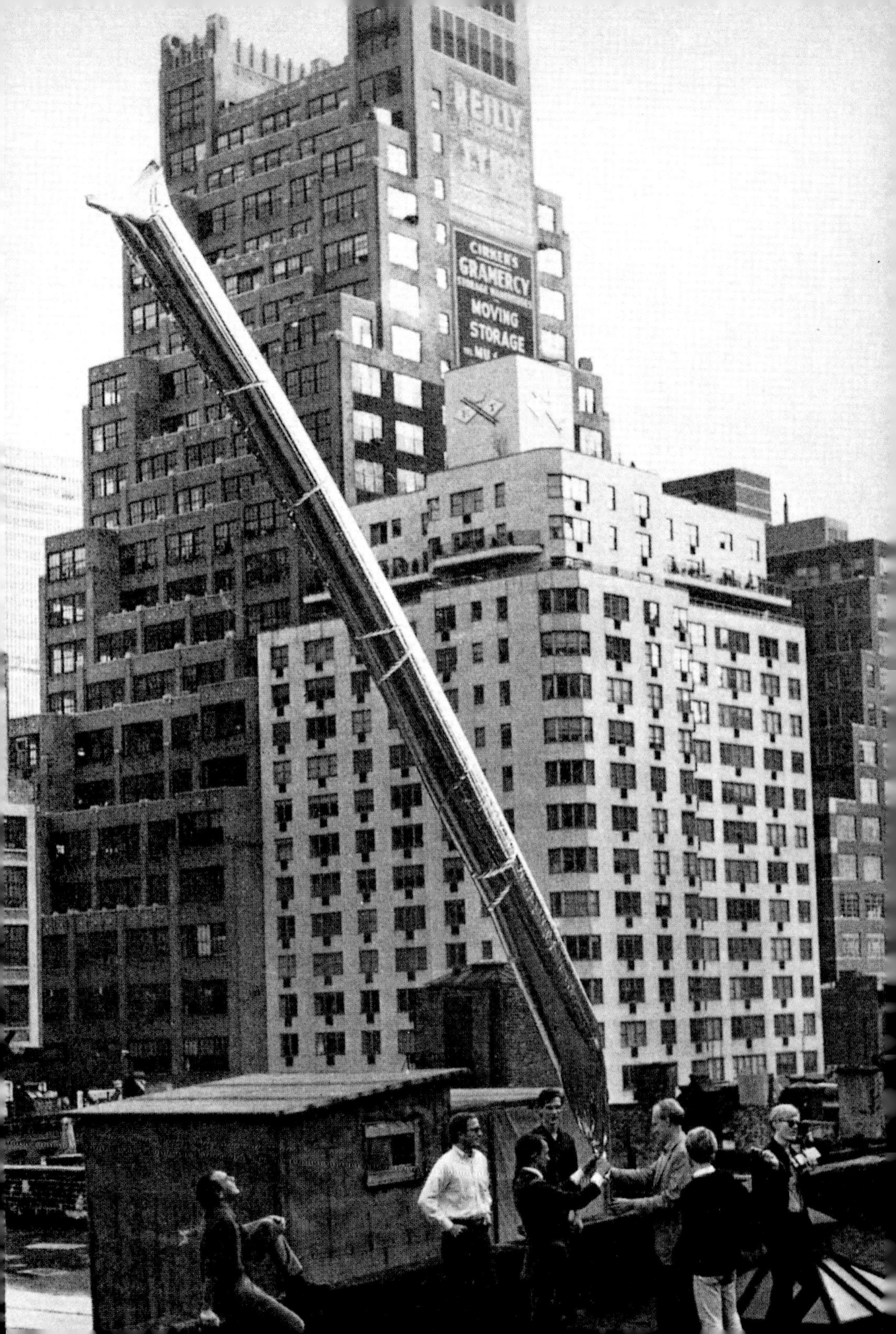
REILLY
CIRKER'S
GRAMERCY
MOVING
STORAGE

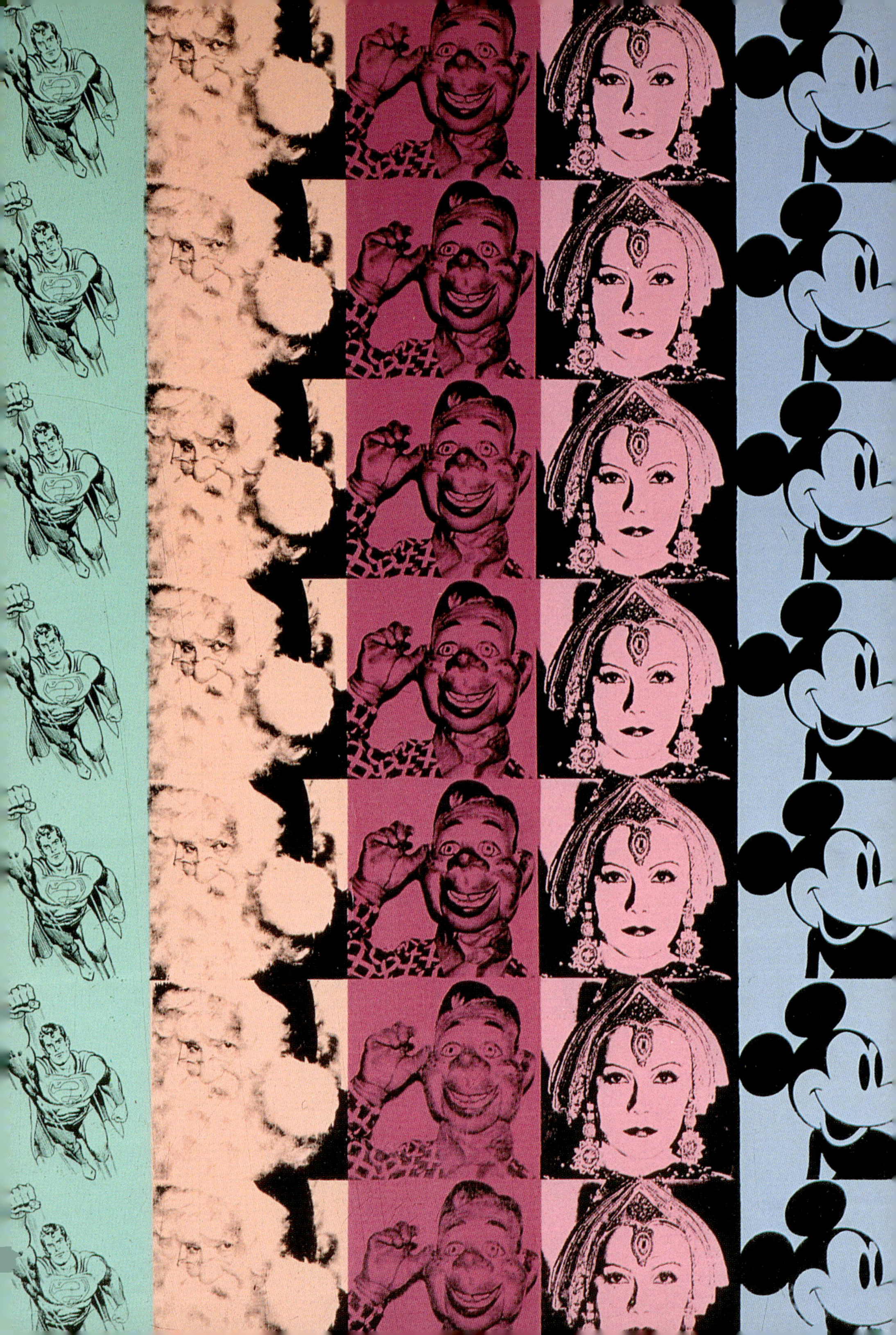

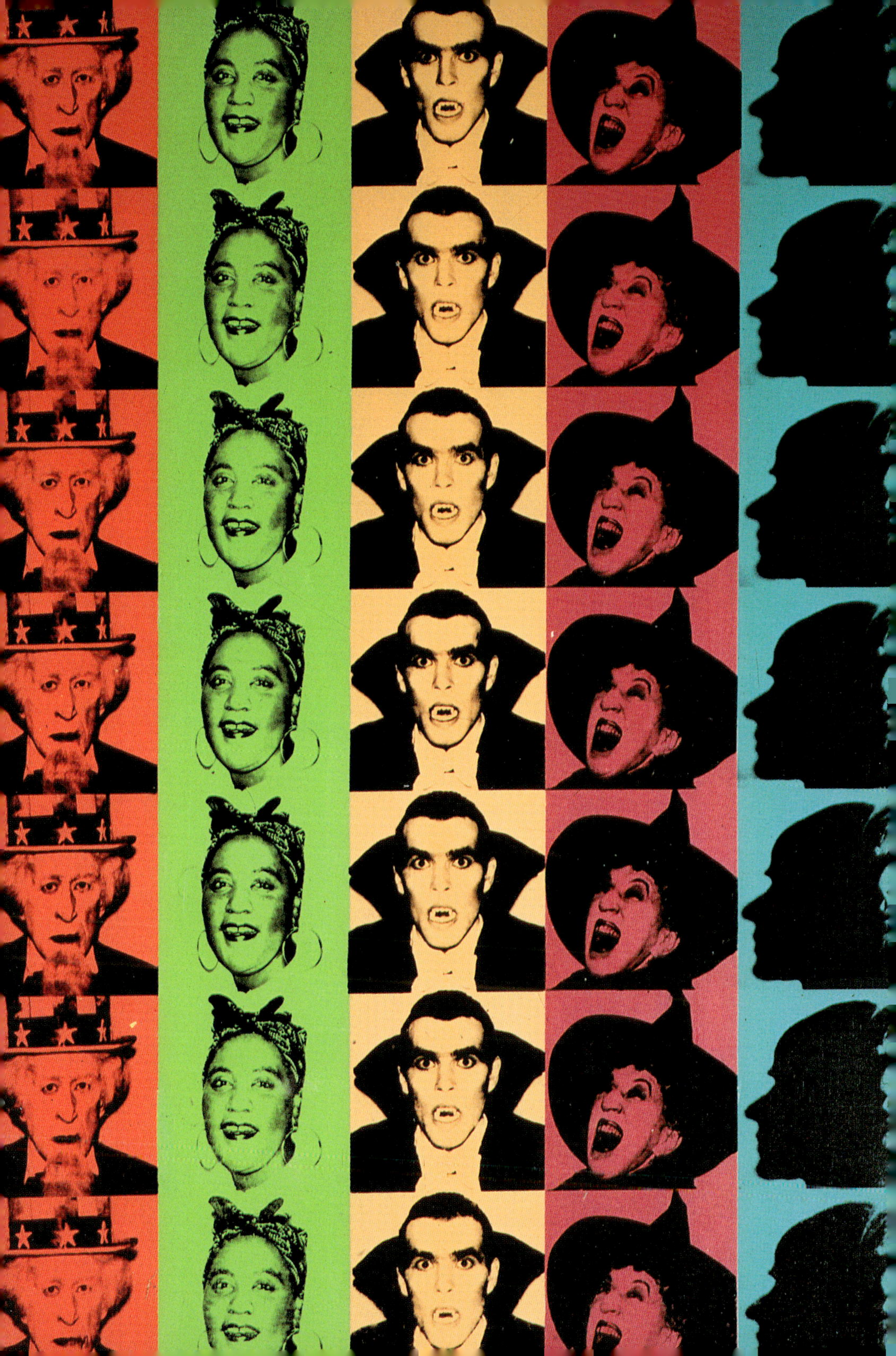

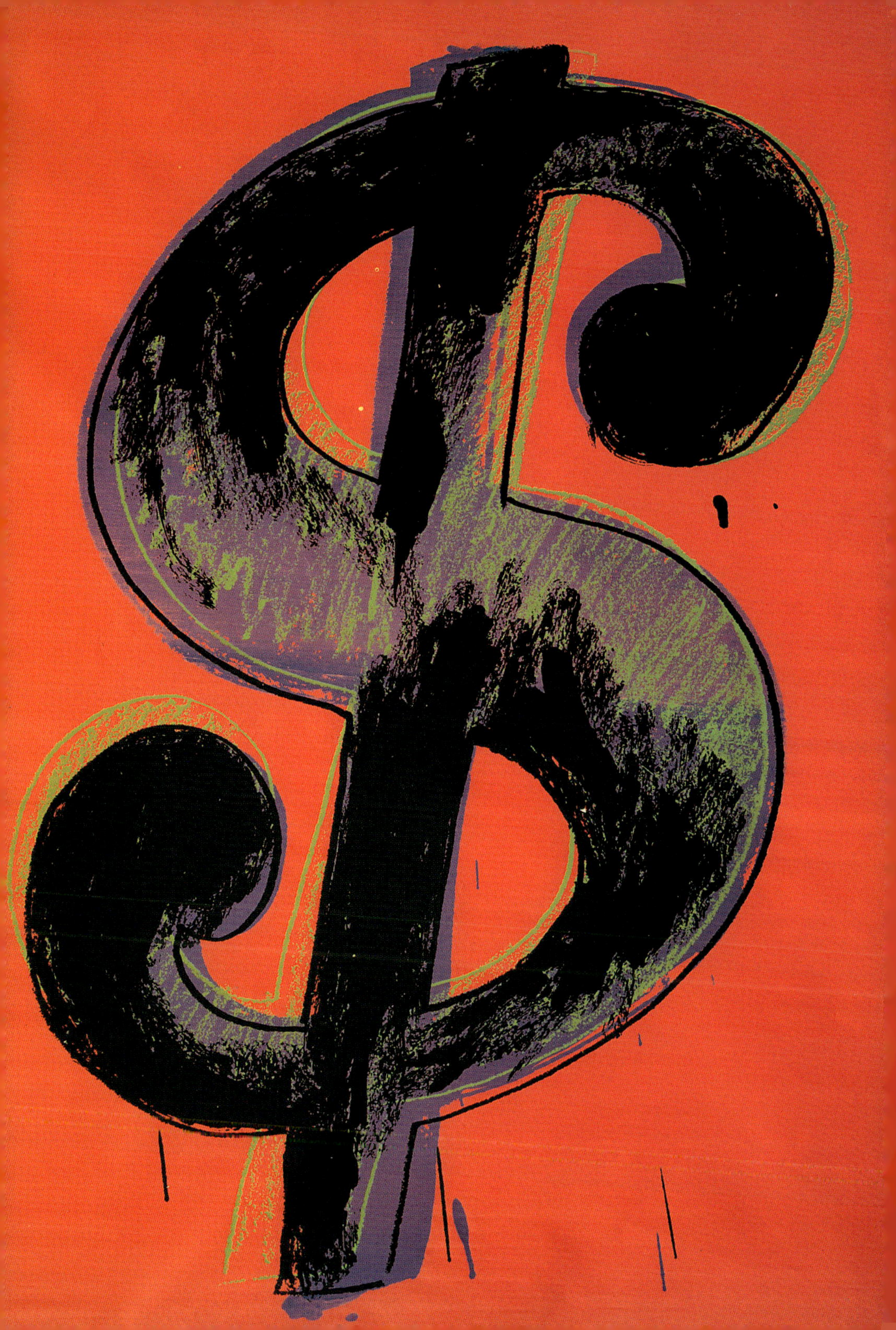

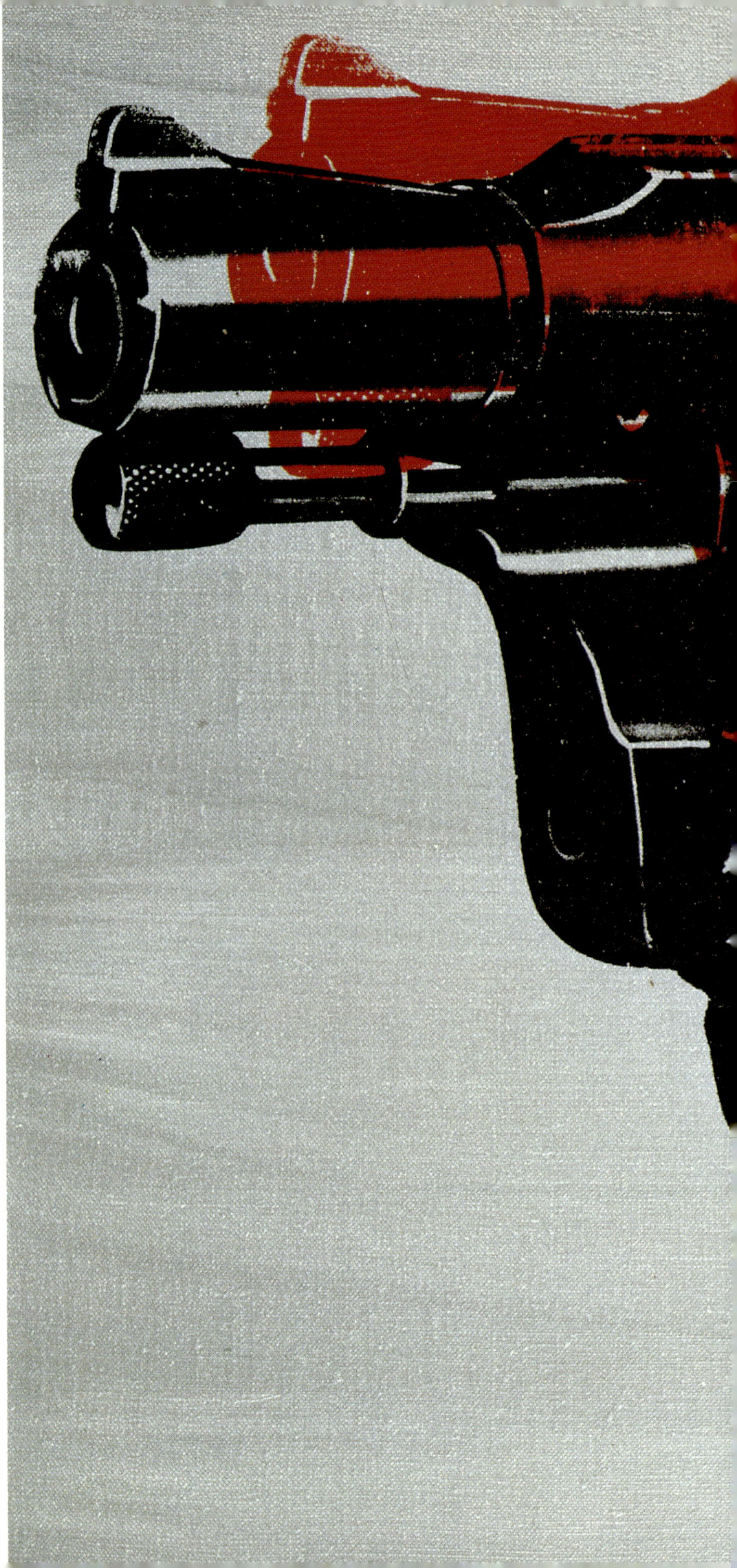

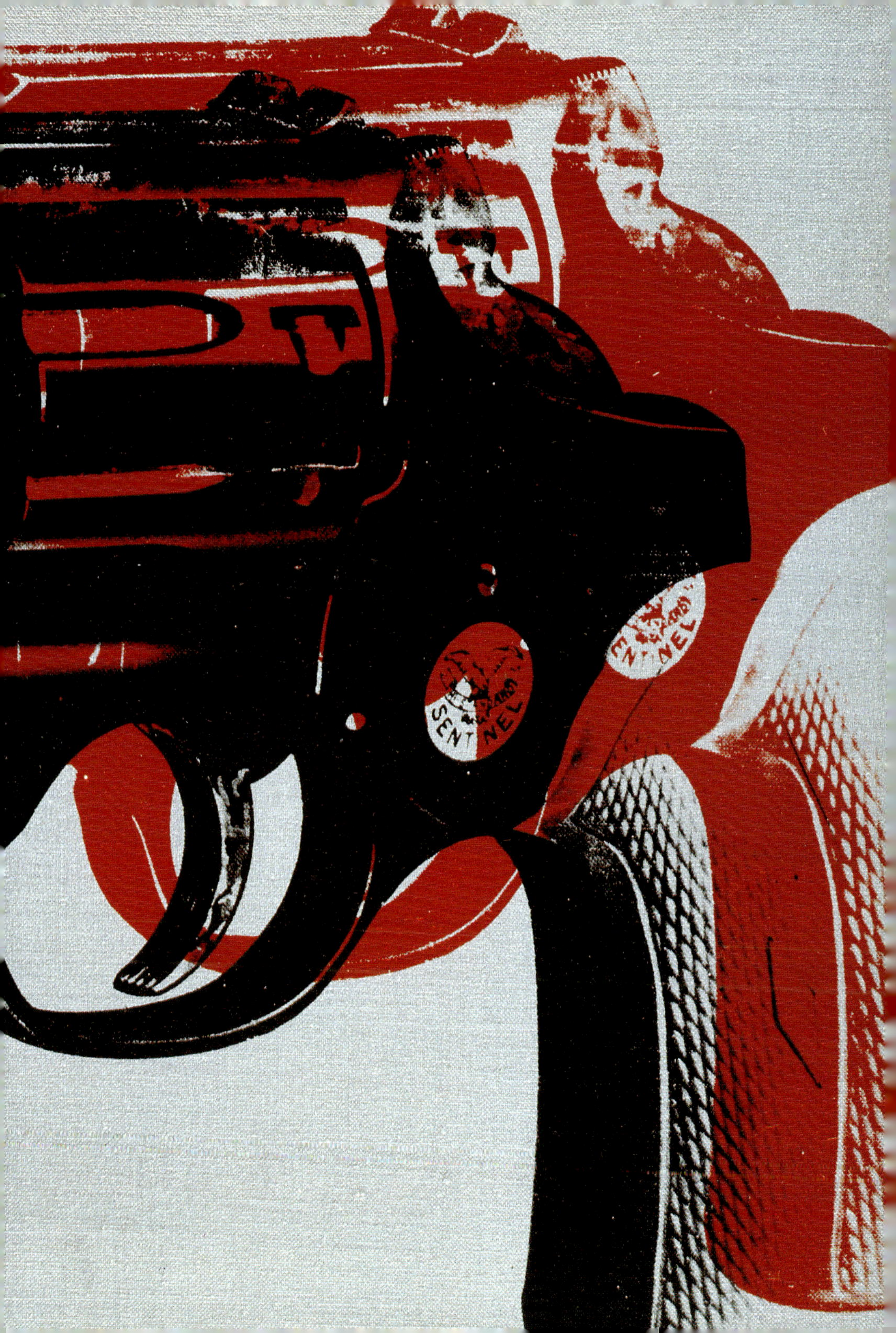

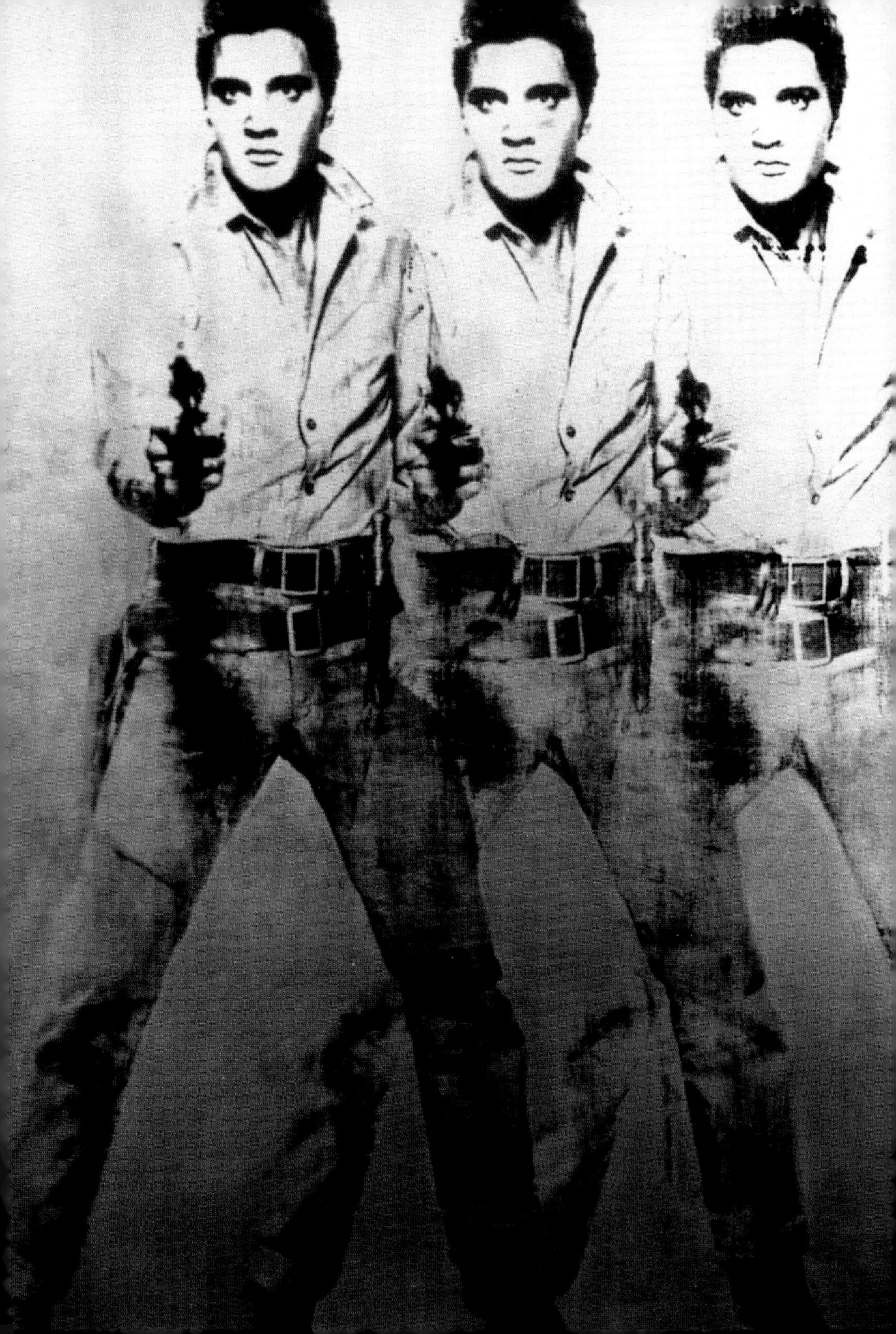

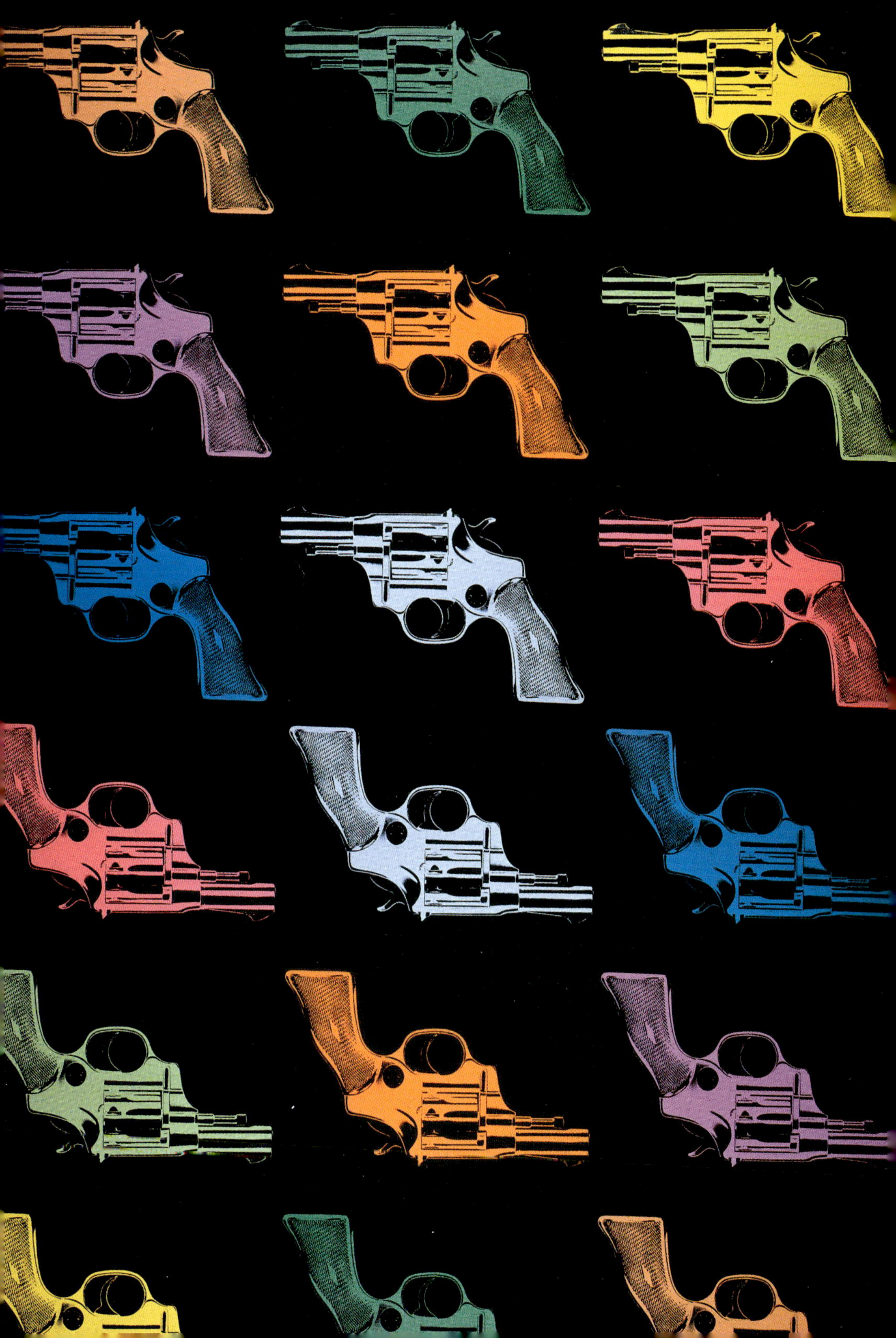

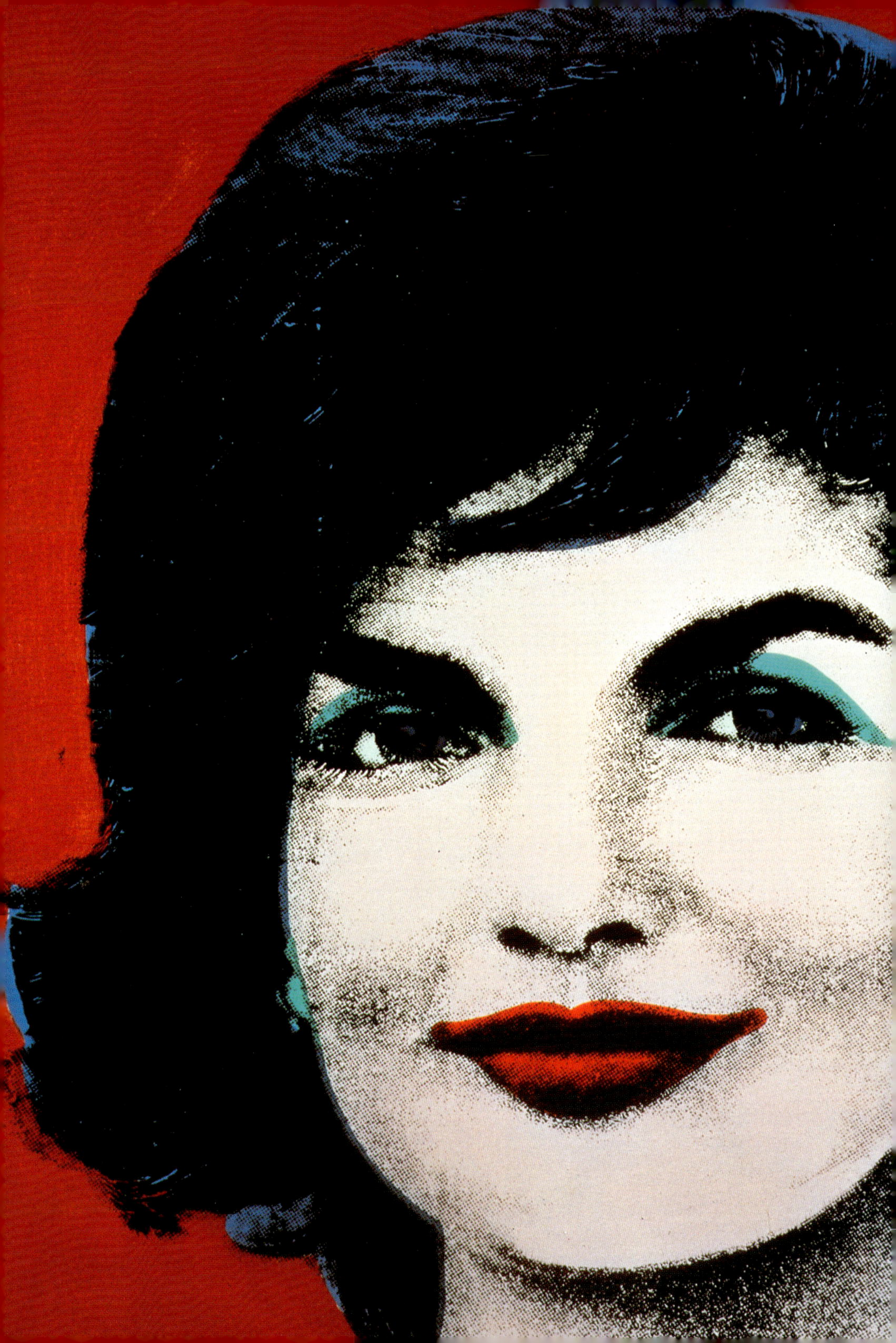

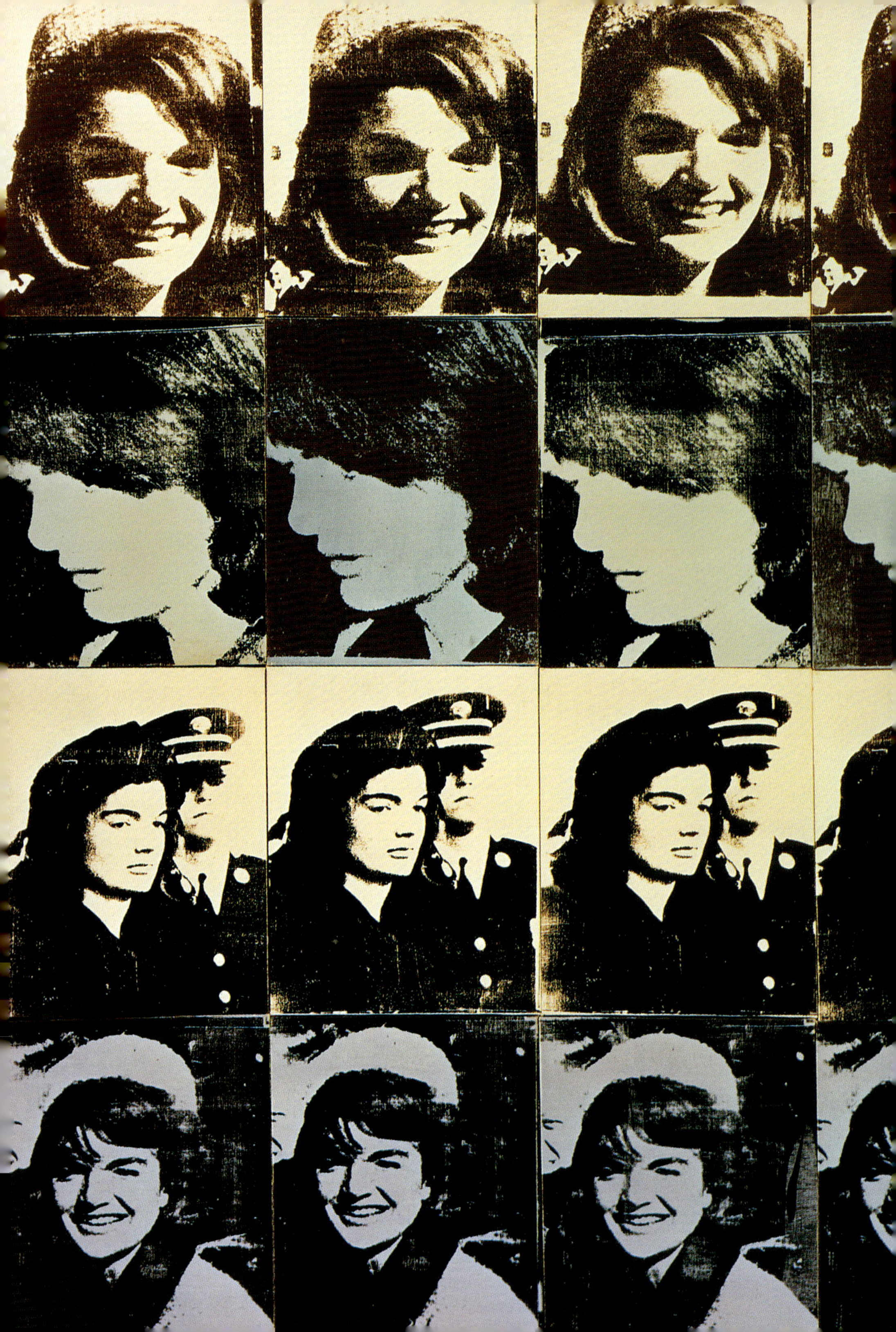

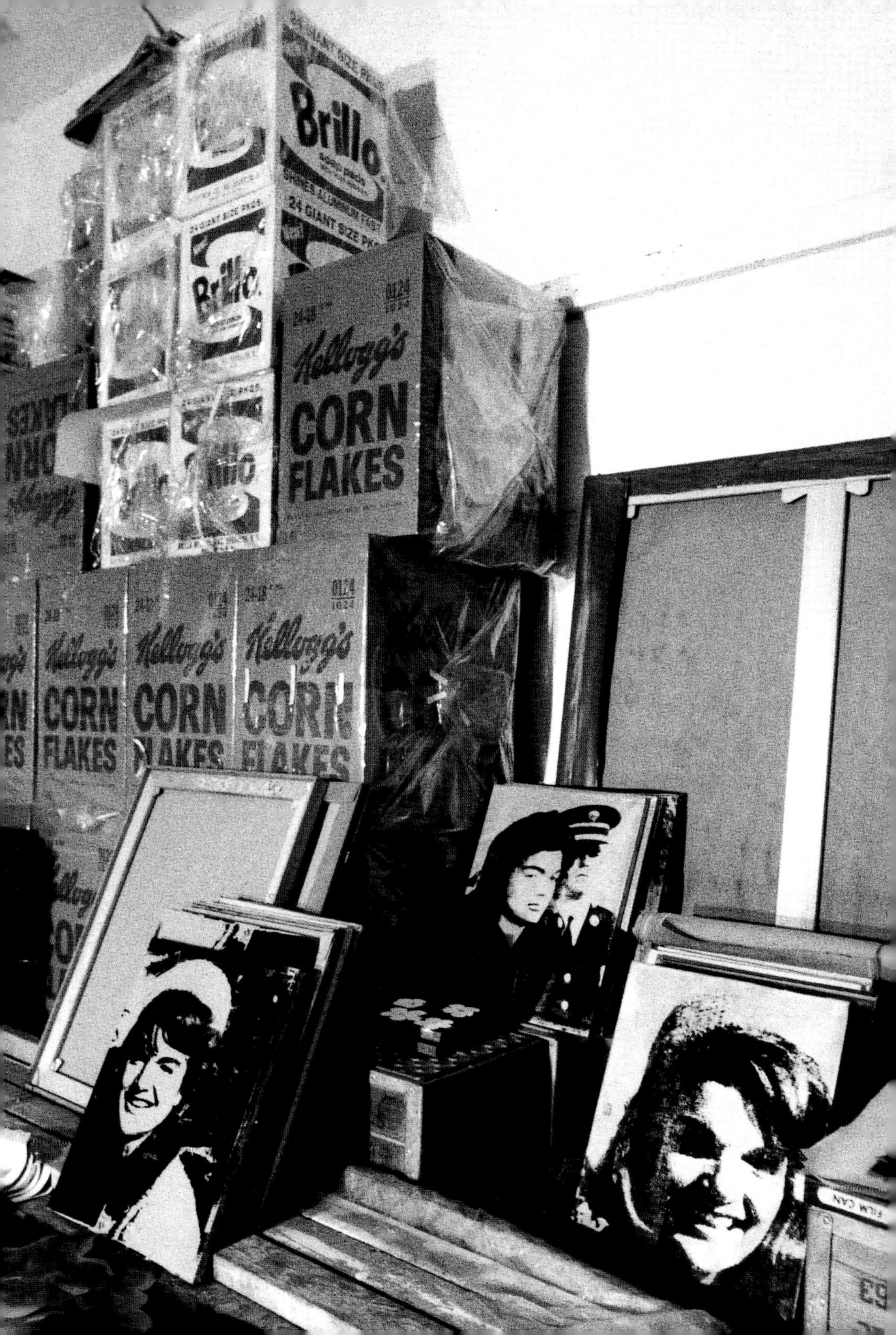

Brillo
SHINES ALUMINUM FAST
24 GIANT SIZE PKGS.
Kellogg's
CORN
FLAKES

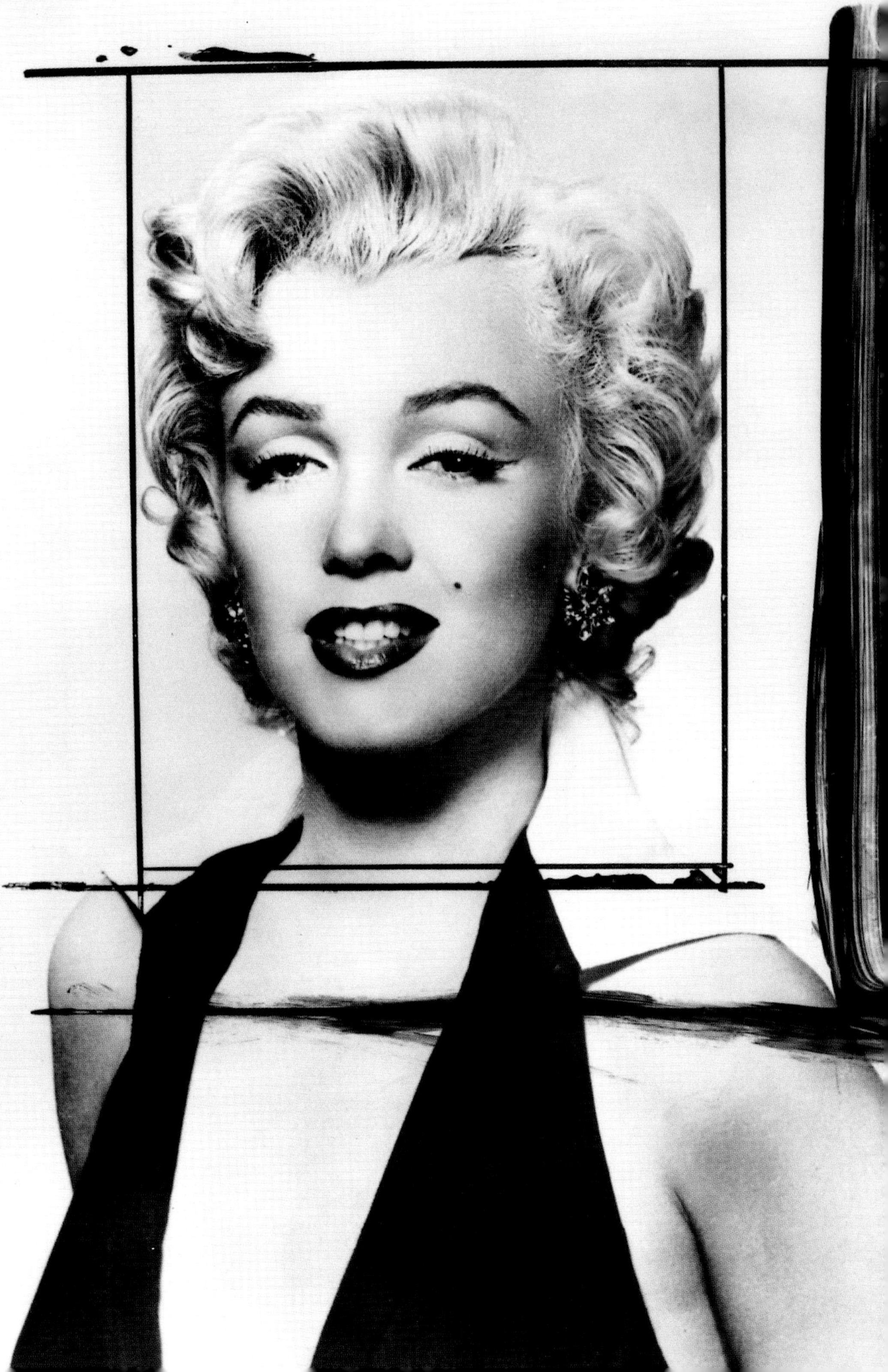

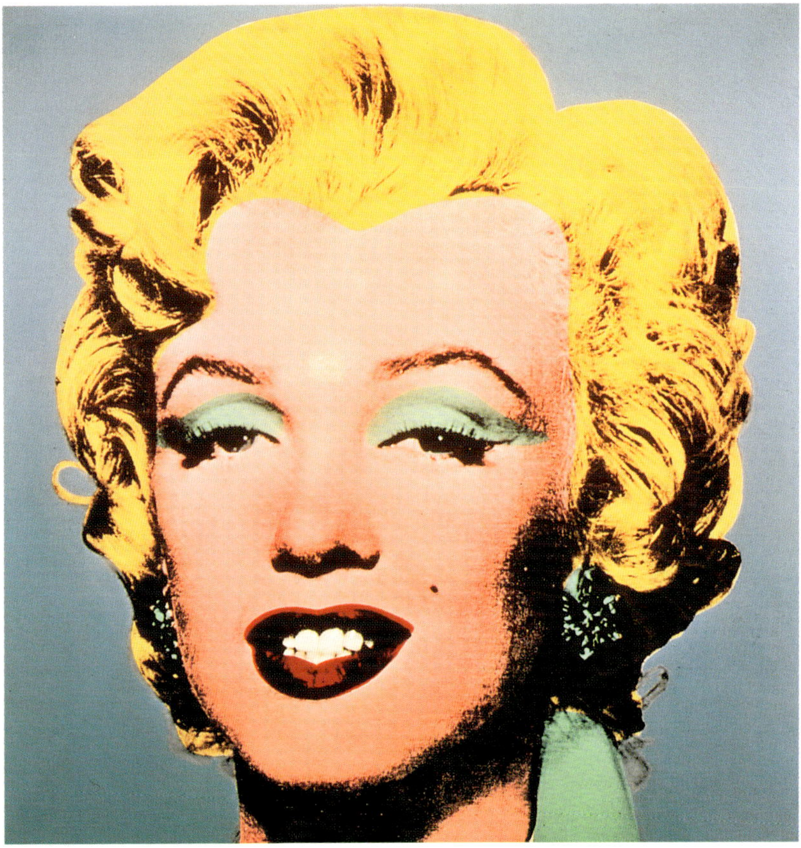

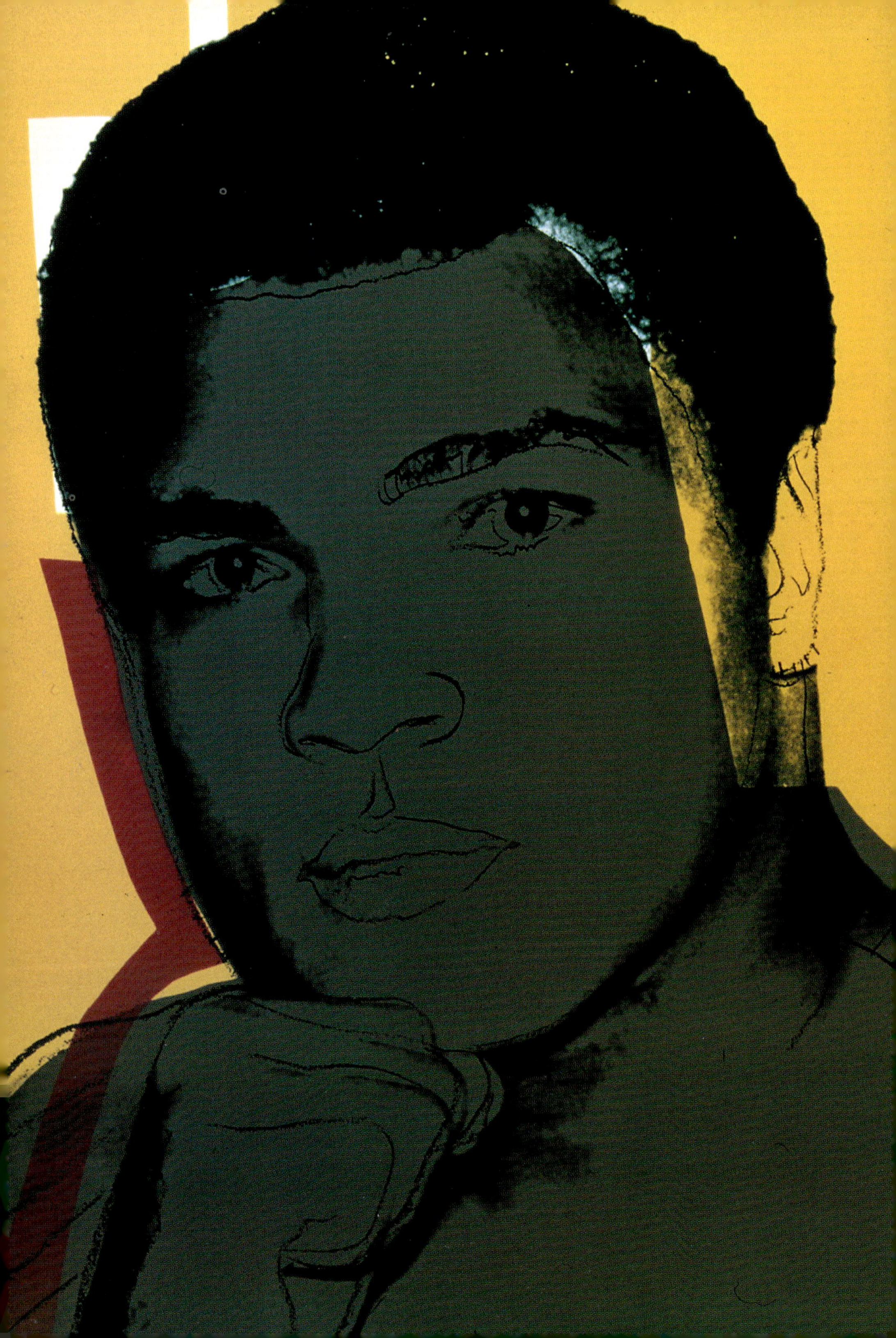

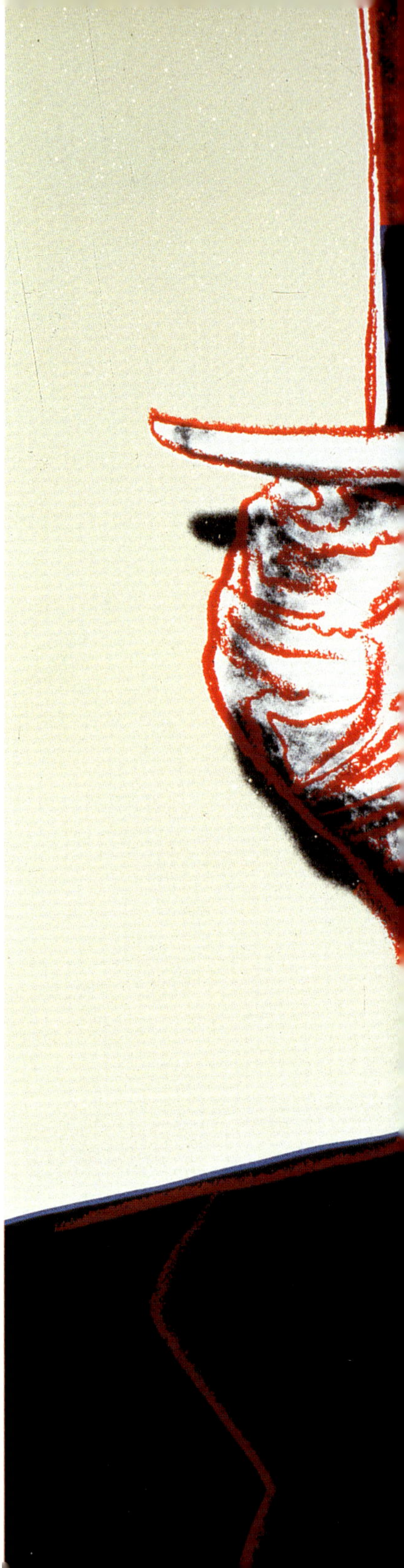

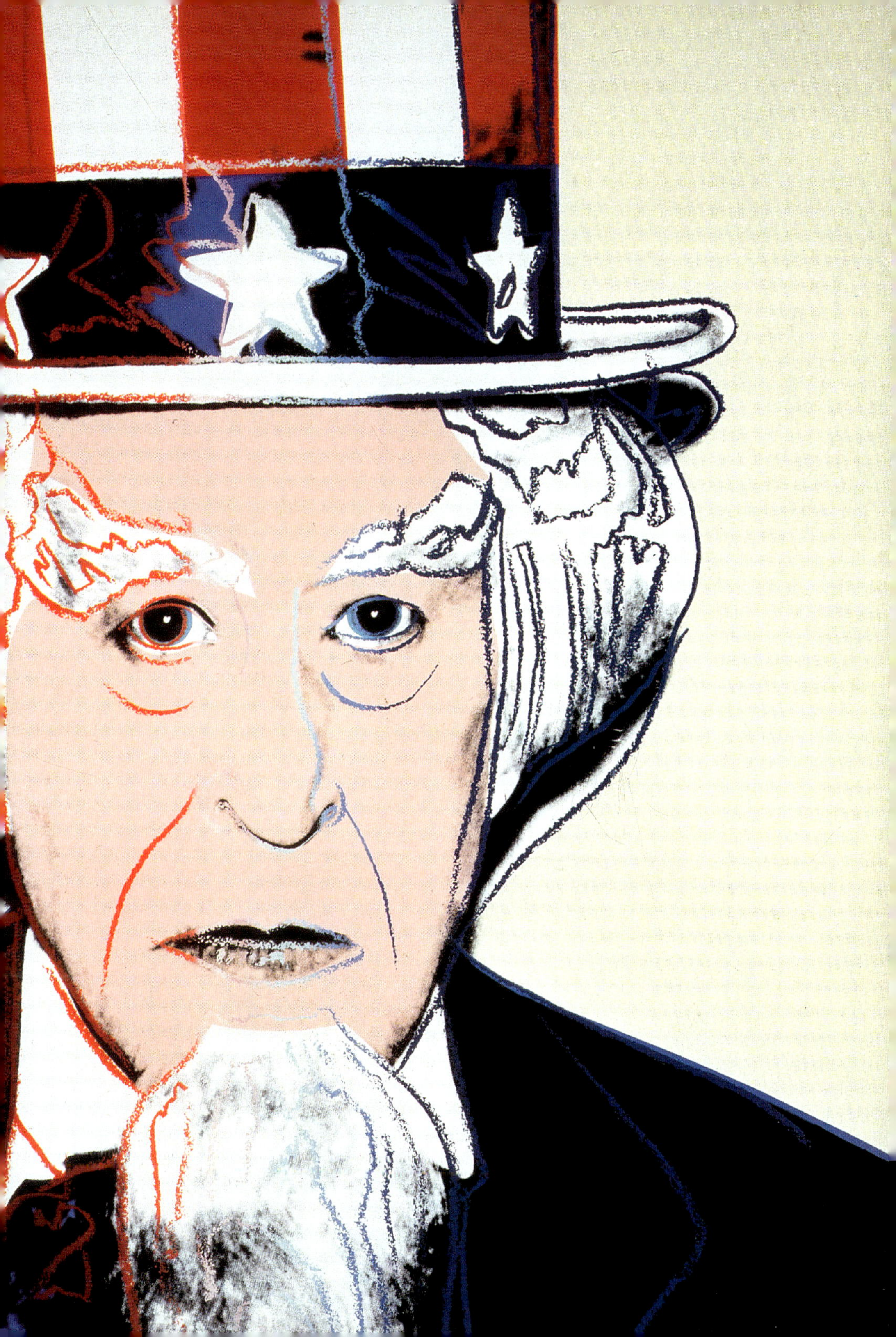

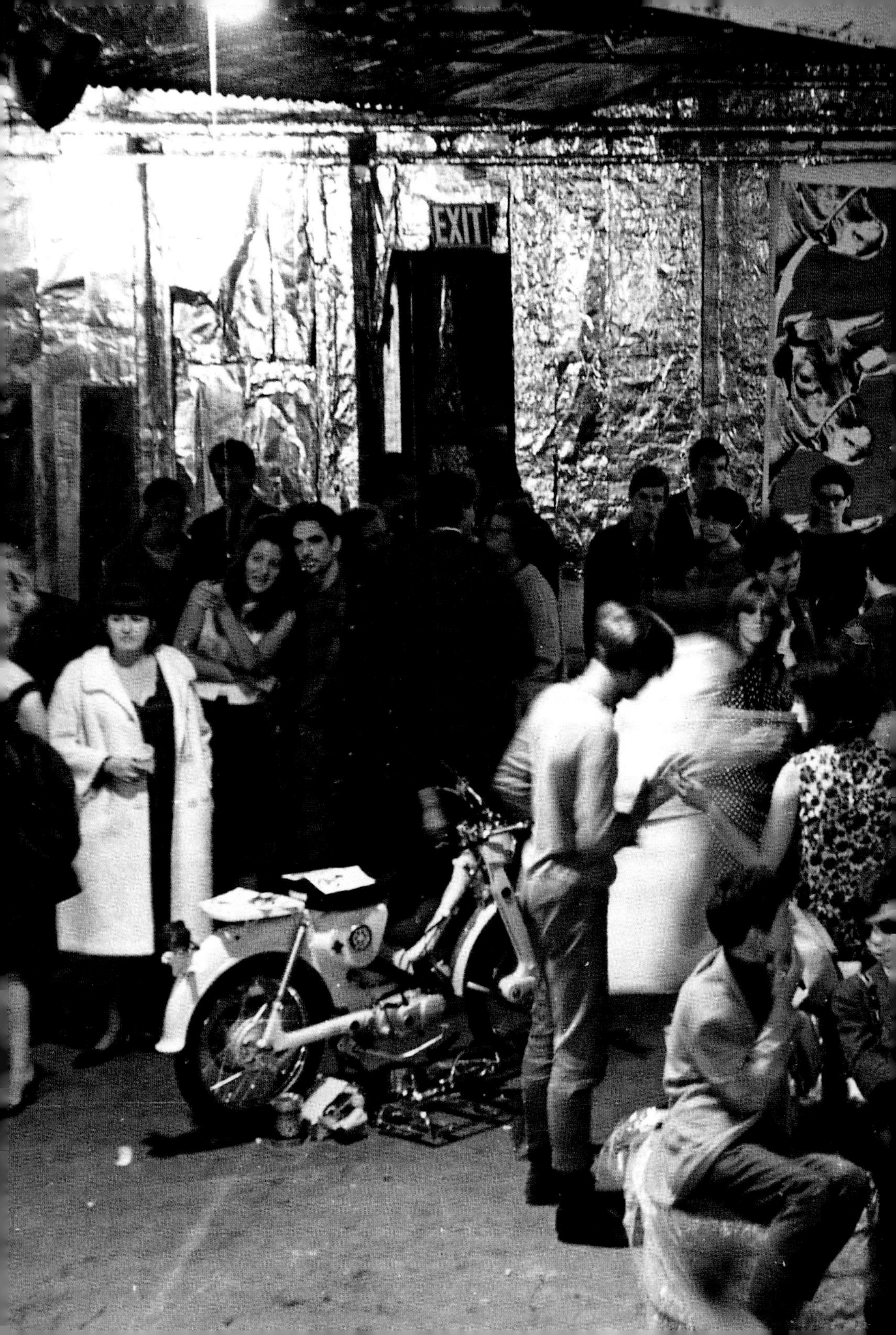
EXIT

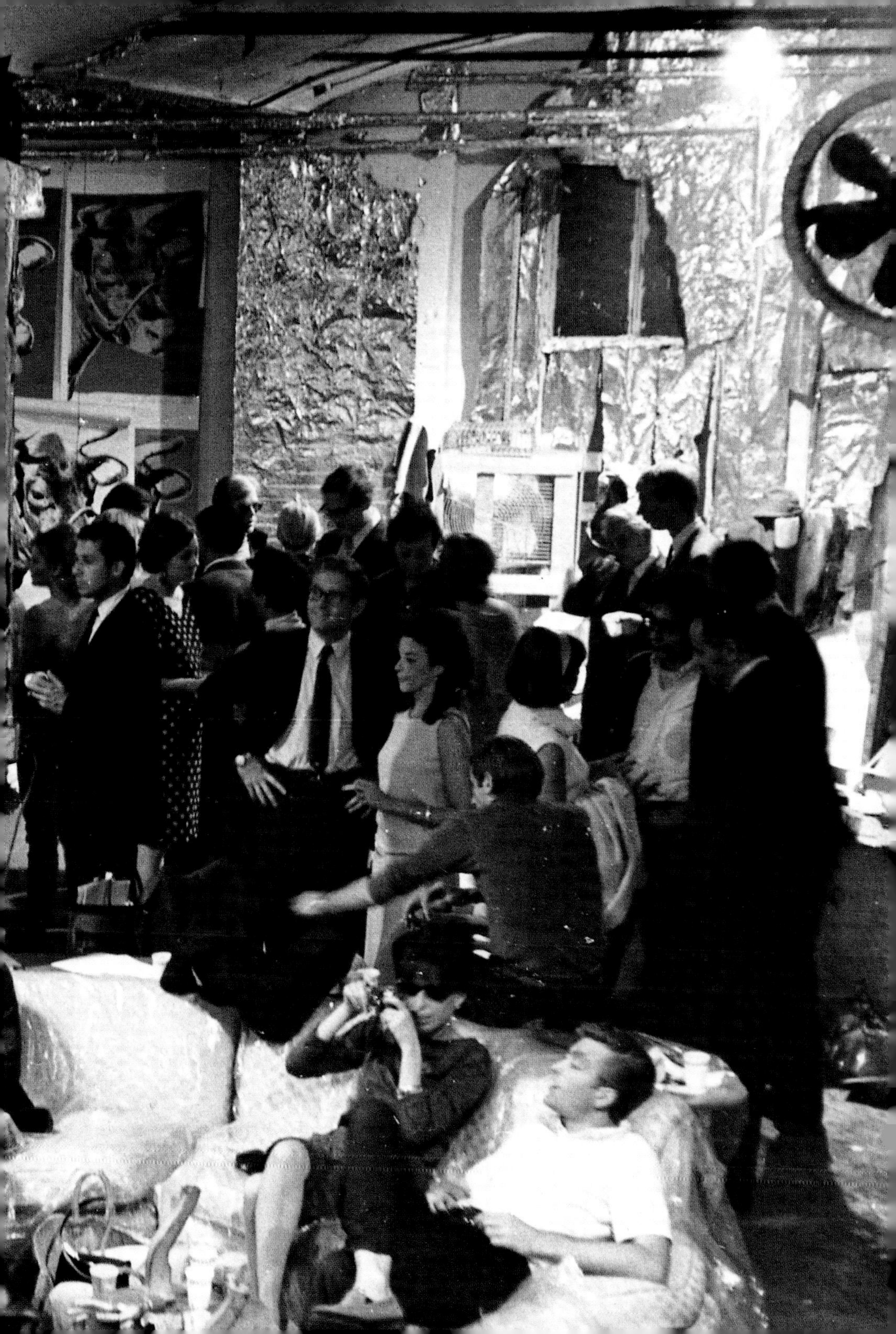

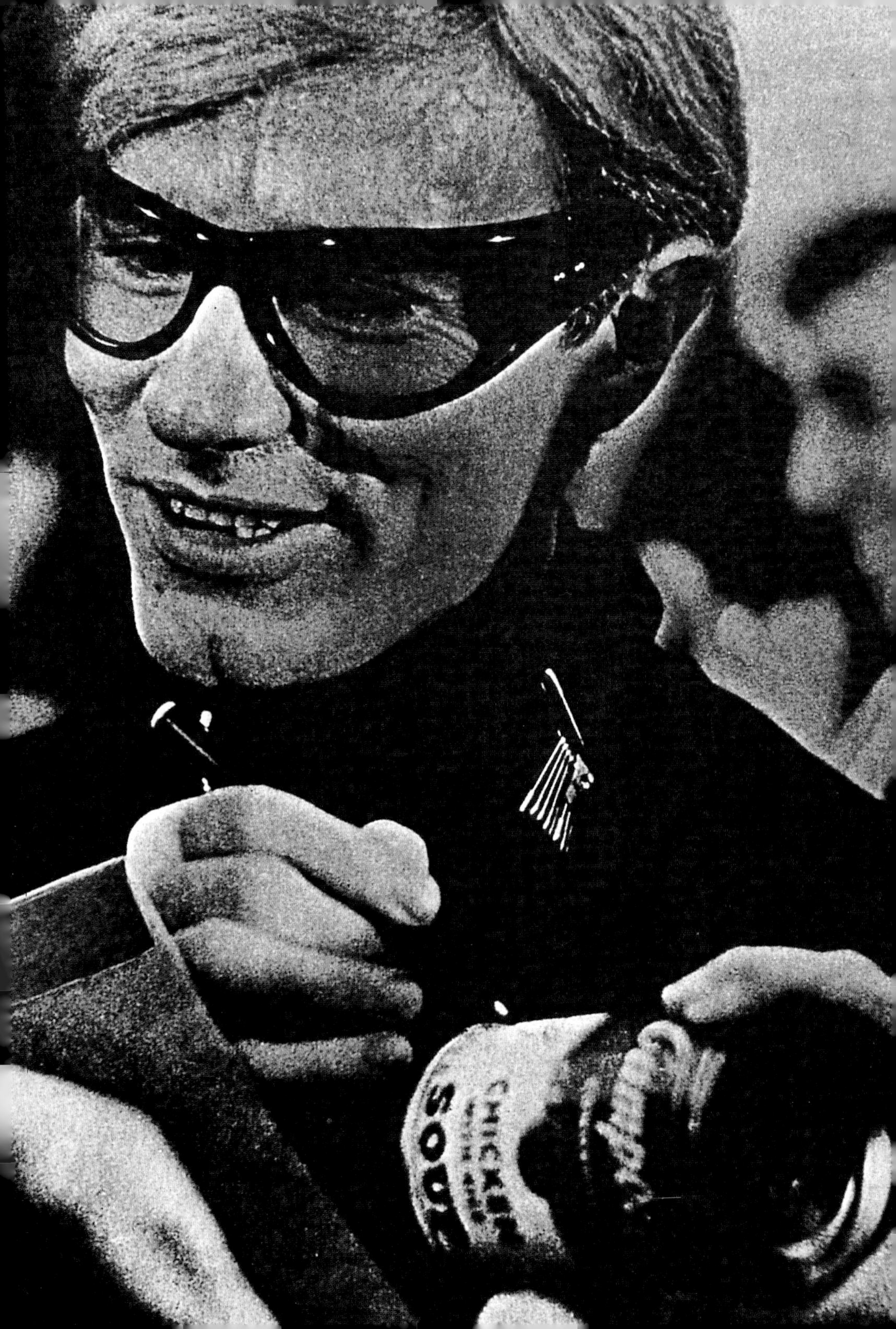

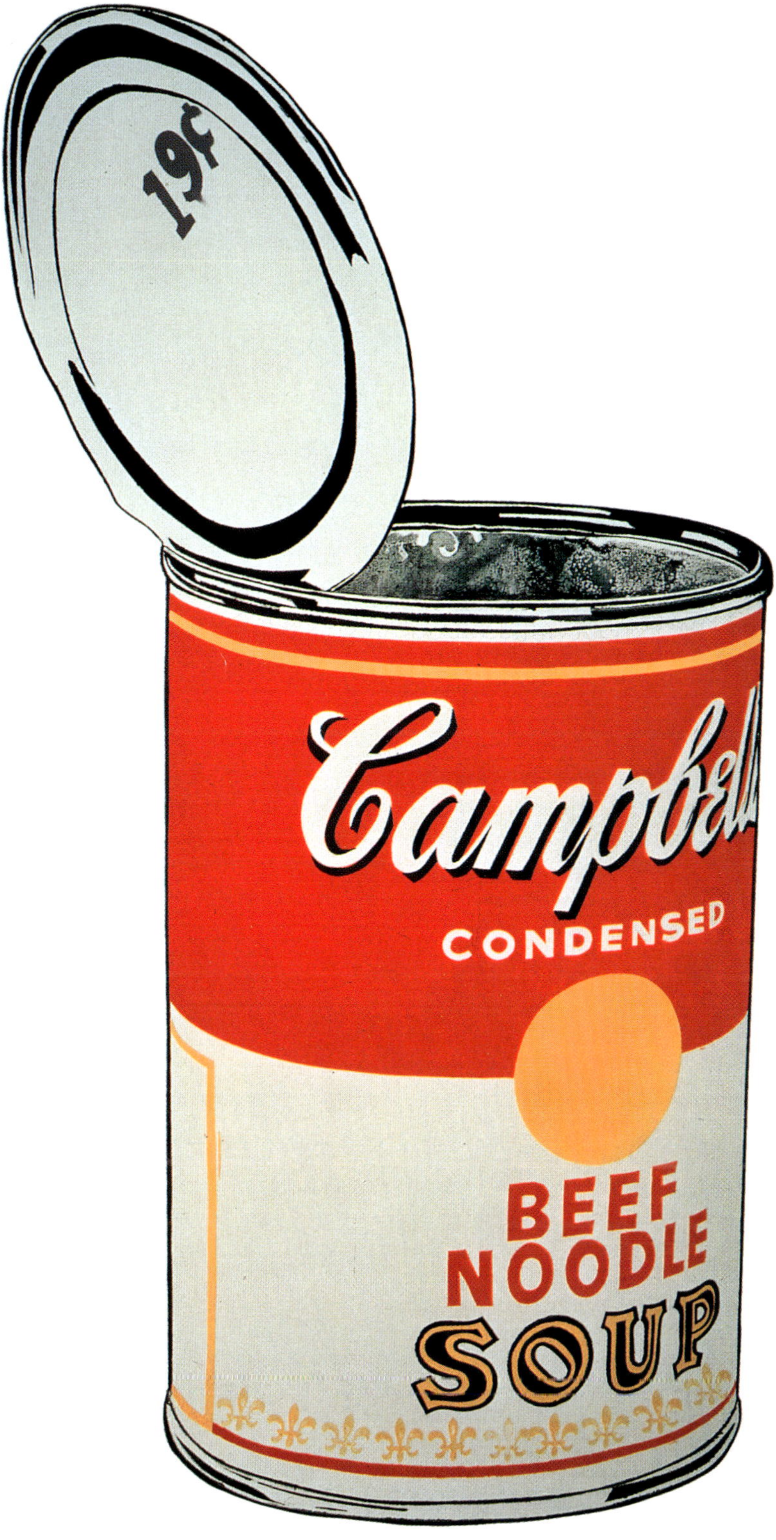
19¢
Campbell's
CONDENSED
BEEF
NOODLE
SOUP

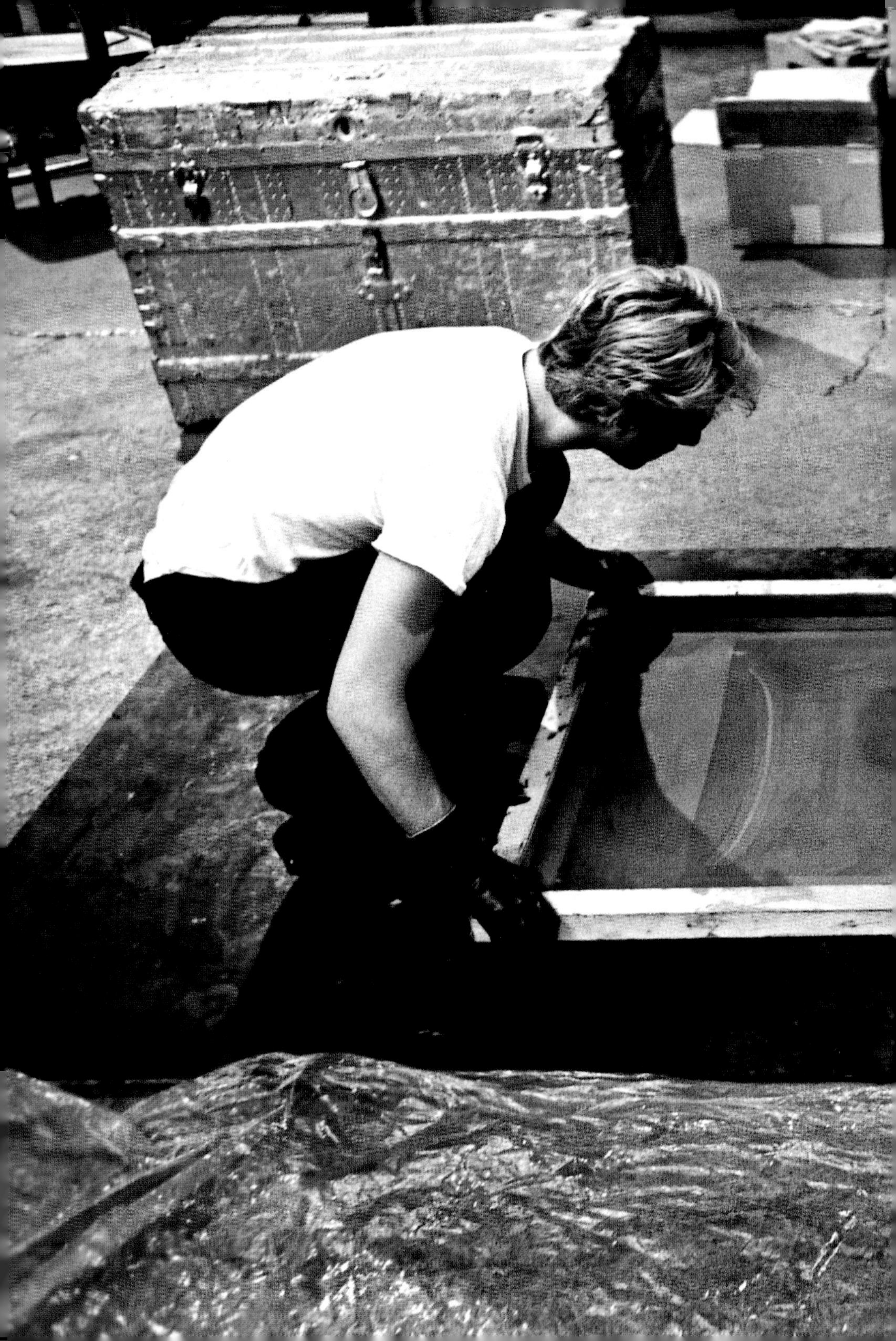

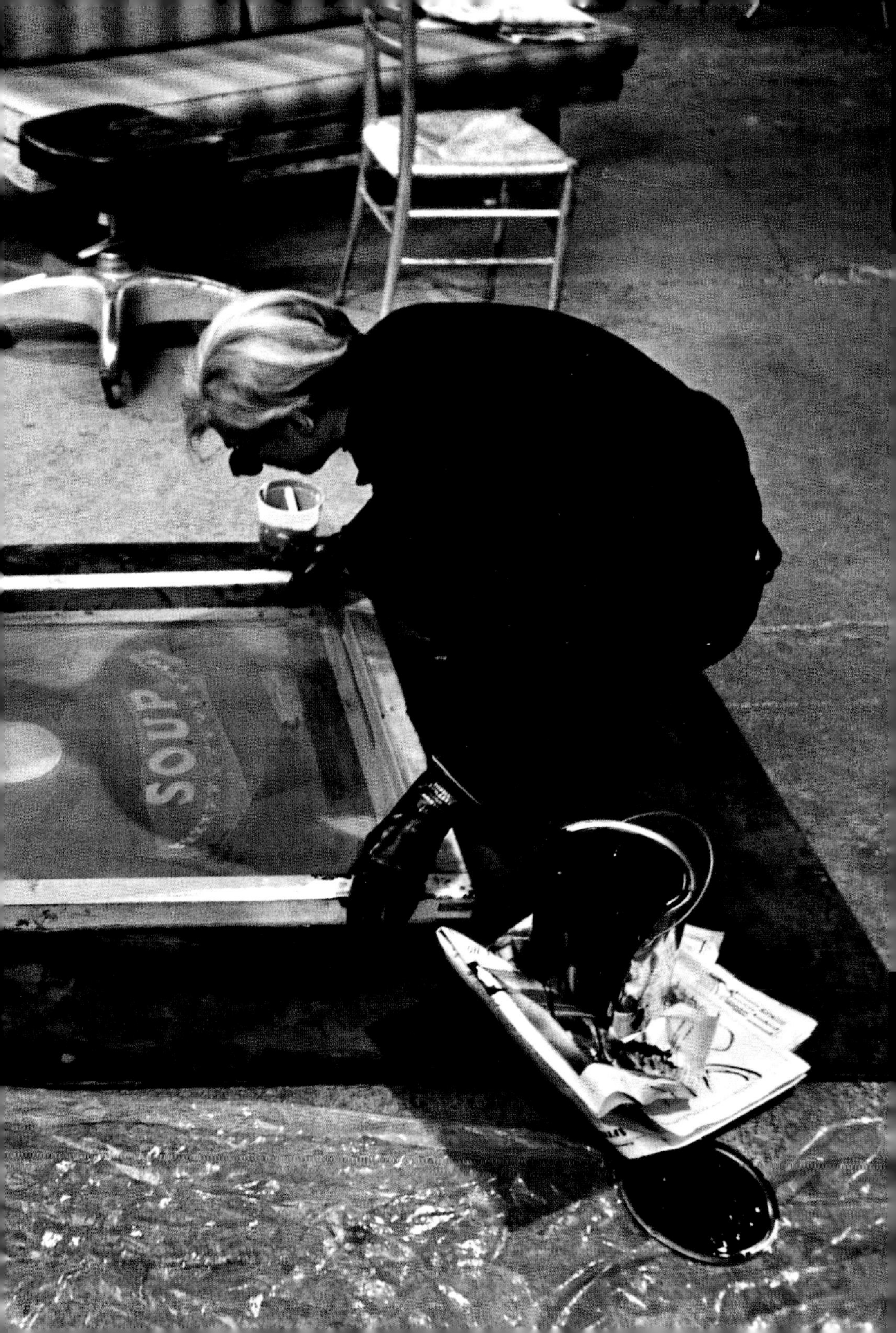
SOUP

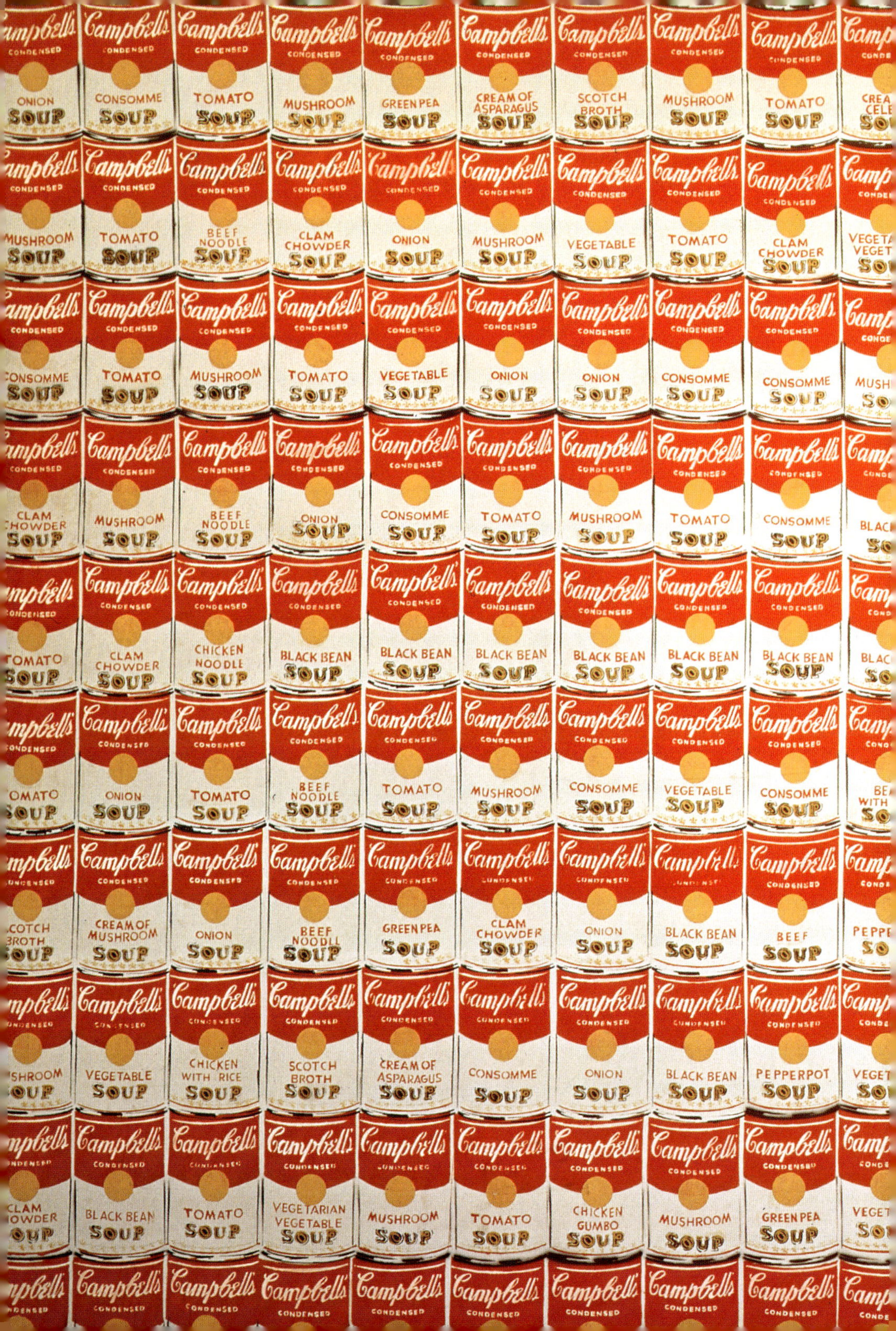
Campbell's CONDENSED CONSOMME SOUP
Campbell's CONDENSED TOMATO SOUP
Campbell's CONDENSED MUSHROOM SOUP
Campbell's CONDENSED GREEN PEA SOUP
Campbell's CONDENSED CREAM OF ASPARAGUS SOUP
Campbell's CONDENSED SCOTCH BROTH SOUP
Campbell's CONDENSED MUSHROOM SOUP
Campbell's CONDENSED TOMATO SOUP
Campbell's CONDENSED TOMATO SOUP
Campbell's CONDENSED BEEF NOODLE SOUP
Campbell's CONDENSED CLAM CHOWDER SOUP
Campbell's CONDENSED ONION SOUP
Campbell's CONDENSED MUSHROOM SOUP
Campbell's CONDENSED VEGETABLE SOUP
Campbell's CONDENSED TOMATO SOUP
Campbell's CONDENSED CLAM CHOWDER SOUP
Campbell's CONDENSED TOMATO SOUP
Campbell's CONDENSED MUSHROOM SOUP
Campbell's CONDENSED TOMATO SOUP
Campbell's CONDENSED VEGETABLE SOUP
Campbell's CONDENSED ONION SOUP
Campbell's CONDENSED ONION SOUP
Campbell's CONDENSED CONSOMME SOUP
Campbell's CONDENSED CONSOMME SOUP
Campbell's CONDENSED MUSHROOM SOUP
Campbell's CONDENSED BEEF NOODLE SOUP
Campbell's CONDENSED ONION SOUP
Campbell's CONDENSED CONSOMME SOUP
Campbell's CONDENSED TOMATO SOUP
Campbell's CONDENSED MUSHROOM SOUP
Campbell's CONDENSED TOMATO SOUP
Campbell's CONDENSED CONSOMME SOUP
Campbell's CONDENSED CLAM CHOWDER SOUP
Campbell's CONDENSED CHICKEN NOODLE SOUP
Campbell's CONDENSED BLACK BEAN SOUP
Campbell's CONDENSED BLACK BEAN SOUP
Campbell's CONDENSED BLACK BEAN SOUP
Campbell's CONDENSED BLACK BEAN SOUP
Campbell's CONDENSED BLACK BEAN SOUP
Campbell's CONDENSED BLACK BEAN SOUP
Campbell's CONDENSED ONION SOUP
Campbell's CONDENSED TOMATO SOUP
Campbell's CONDENSED BEEF NOODLE SOUP
Campbell's CONDENSED TOMATO SOUP
Campbell's CONDENSED MUSHROOM SOUP
Campbell's CONDENSED CONSOMME SOUP
Campbell's CONDENSED VEGETABLE SOUP
Campbell's CONDENSED CONSOMME SOUP
Campbell's CONDENSED CREAM OF MUSHROOM SOUP
Campbell's CONDENSED ONION SOUP
Campbell's CONDENSED BEEF NOODLE SOUP
Campbell's CONDENSED GREEN PEA SOUP
Campbell's CONDENSED CLAM CHOWDER SOUP
Campbell's CONDENSED ONION SOUP
Campbell's CONDENSED BLACK BEAN SOUP
Campbell's CONDENSED BEEF SOUP
Campbell's CONDENSED VEGETABLE SOUP
Campbell's CONDENSED CHICKEN WITH RICE SOUP
Campbell's CONDENSED SCOTCH BROTH SOUP
Campbell's CONDENSED CREAM OF ASPARAGUS SOUP
Campbell's CONDENSED CONSOMME SOUP
Campbell's CONDENSED ONION SOUP
Campbell's CONDENSED BLACK BEAN SOUP
Campbell's CONDENSED PEPPERPOT SOUP
Campbell's CONDENSED BLACK BEAN SOUP
Campbell's CONDENSED TOMATO SOUP
Campbell's CONDENSED VEGETARIAN VEGETABLE SOUP
Campbell's CONDENSED MUSHROOM SOUP
Campbell's CONDENSED TOMATO SOUP
Campbell's CONDENSED CHICKEN GUMBO SOUP
Campbell's CONDENSED MUSHROOM SOUP
Campbell's CONDENSED GREEN PEA SOUP

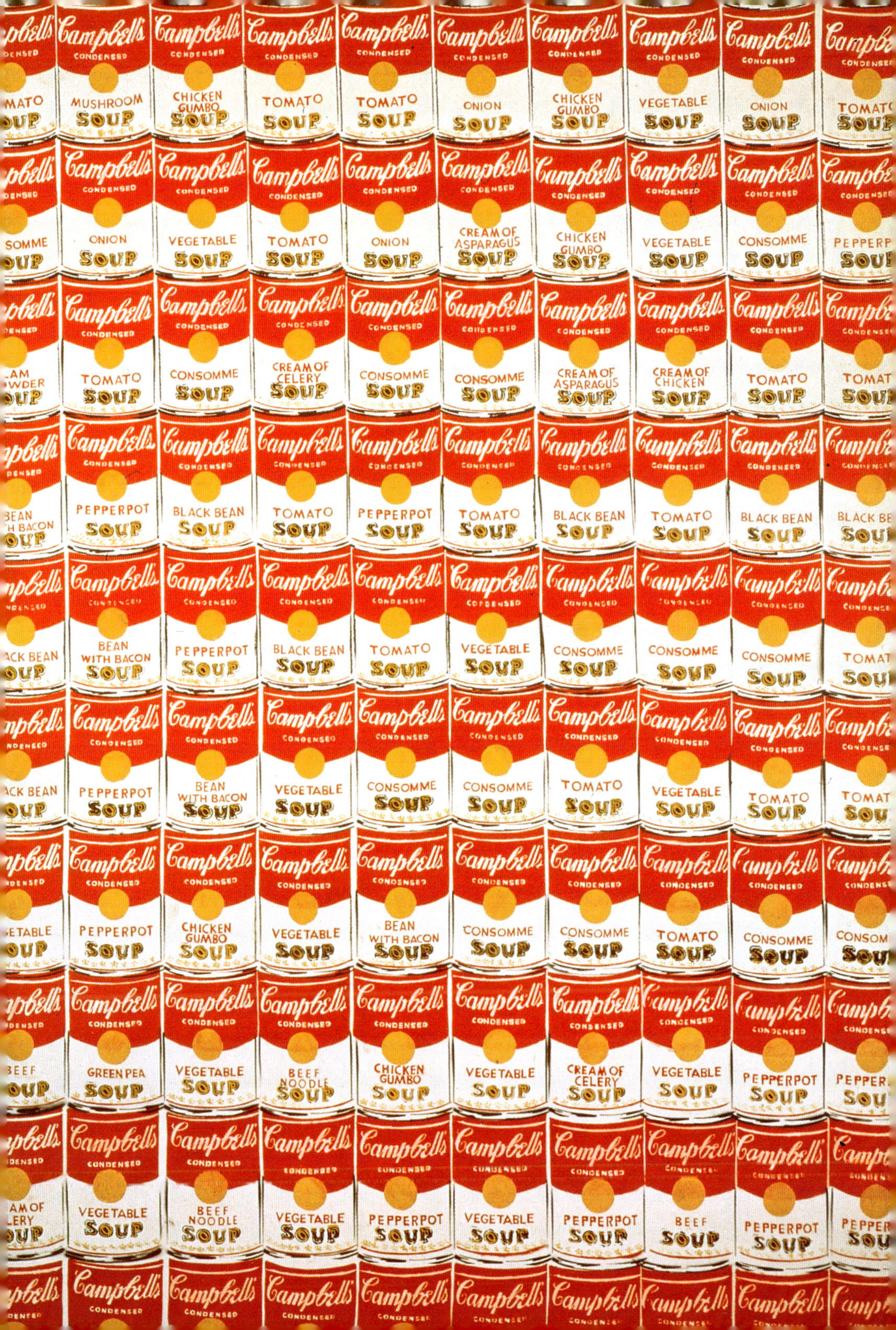
Campbell's CONDENSED MUSHROOM SOUP
Campbell's CONDENSED CHICKEN GUMBO SOUP
Campbell's CONDENSED TOMATO SOUP
Campbell's CONDENSED TOMATO SOUP
Campbell's CONDENSED ONION SOUP
Campbell's CONDENSED CHICKEN GUMBO SOUP
Campbell's CONDENSED VEGETABLE SOUP
Campbell's CONDENSED ONION SOUP
Campbell's CONDENSED ONION SOUP
Campbell's CONDENSED VEGETABLE SOUP
Campbell's CONDENSED TOMATO SOUP
Campbell's CONDENSED ONION SOUP
Campbell's CONDENSED CREAM OF ASPARAGUS SOUP
Campbell's CONDENSED CHICKEN GUMBO SOUP
Campbell's CONDENSED VEGETABLE SOUP
Campbell's CONDENSED CONSOMME SOUP
Campbell's CONDENSED TOMATO SOUP
Campbell's CONDENSED CONSOMME SOUP
Campbell's CONDENSED CREAM OF CELERY SOUP
Campbell's CONDENSED CONSOMME SOUP
Campbell's CONDENSED CONSOMME SOUP
Campbell's CONDENSED CREAM OF ASPARAGUS SOUP
Campbell's CONDENSED CREAM OF CHICKEN SOUP
Campbell's CONDENSED TOMATO SOUP
Campbell's CONDENSED PEPPERPOT SOUP
Campbell's CONDENSED BLACK BEAN SOUP
Campbell's CONDENSED TOMATO SOUP
Campbell's CONDENSED PEPPERPOT SOUP
Campbell's CONDENSED TOMATO SOUP
Campbell's CONDENSED BLACK BEAN SOUP
Campbell's CONDENSED TOMATO SOUP
Campbell's CONDENSED BLACK BEAN SOUP
Campbell's CONDENSED BEAN WITH BACON SOUP
Campbell's CONDENSED PEPPERPOT SOUP
Campbell's CONDENSED BLACK BEAN SOUP
Campbell's CONDENSED TOMATO SOUP
Campbell's CONDENSED VEGETABLE SOUP
Campbell's CONDENSED CONSOMME SOUP
Campbell's CONDENSED CONSOMME SOUP
Campbell's CONDENSED CONSOMME SOUP
Campbell's CONDENSED PEPPERPOT SOUP
Campbell's CONDENSED BEAN WITH BACON SOUP
Campbell's CONDENSED VEGETABLE SOUP
Campbell's CONDENSED CONSOMME SOUP
Campbell's CONDENSED CONSOMME SOUP
Campbell's CONDENSED TOMATO SOUP
Campbell's CONDENSED VEGETABLE SOUP
Campbell's CONDENSED TOMATO SOUP
Campbell's CONDENSED PEPPERPOT SOUP
Campbell's CONDENSED CHICKEN GUMBO SOUP
Campbell's CONDENSED VEGETABLE SOUP
Campbell's CONDENSED BEAN WITH BACON SOUP
Campbell's CONDENSED CONSOMME SOUP
Campbell's CONDENSED CONSOMME SOUP
Campbell's CONDENSED TOMATO SOUP
Campbell's CONDENSED CONSOMME SOUP
Campbell's CONDENSED GREEN PEA SOUP
Campbell's CONDENSED VEGETABLE SOUP
Campbell's CONDENSED BEEF NOODLE SOUP
Campbell's CONDENSED CHICKEN GUMBO SOUP
Campbell's CONDENSED VEGETABLE SOUP
Campbell's CONDENSED CREAM OF CELERY SOUP
Campbell's CONDENSED VEGETABLE SOUP
Campbell's CONDENSED PEPPERPOT SOUP
Campbell's CONDENSED VEGETABLE SOUP
Campbell's CONDENSED BEEF NOODLE SOUP
Campbell's CONDENSED VEGETABLE SOUP
Campbell's CONDENSED PEPPERPOT SOUP
Campbell's CONDENSED VEGETABLE SOUP
Campbell's CONDENSED PEPPERPOT SOUP
Campbell's CONDENSED BEEF SOUP
Campbell's CONDENSED PEPPERPOT SOUP

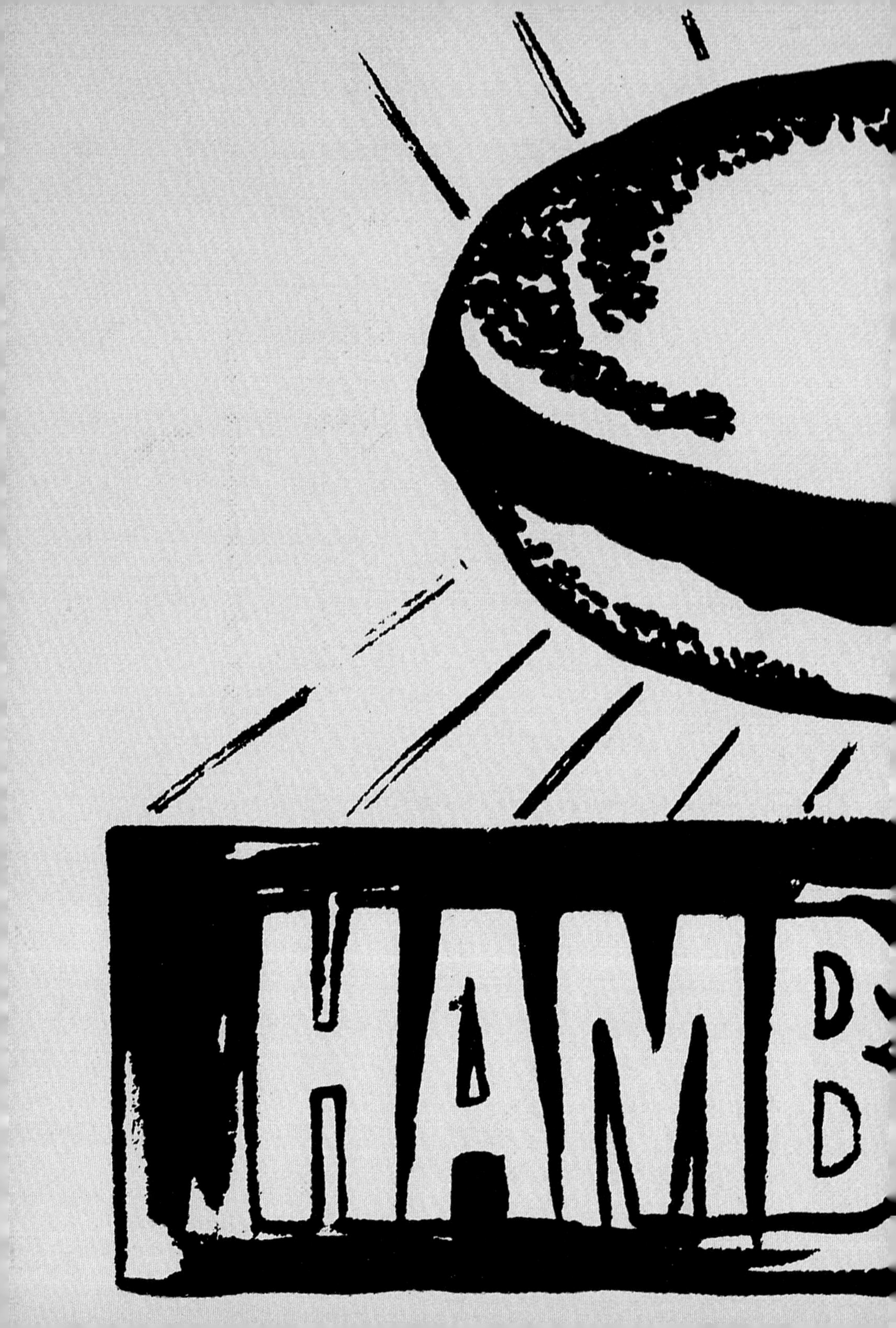
HAMB

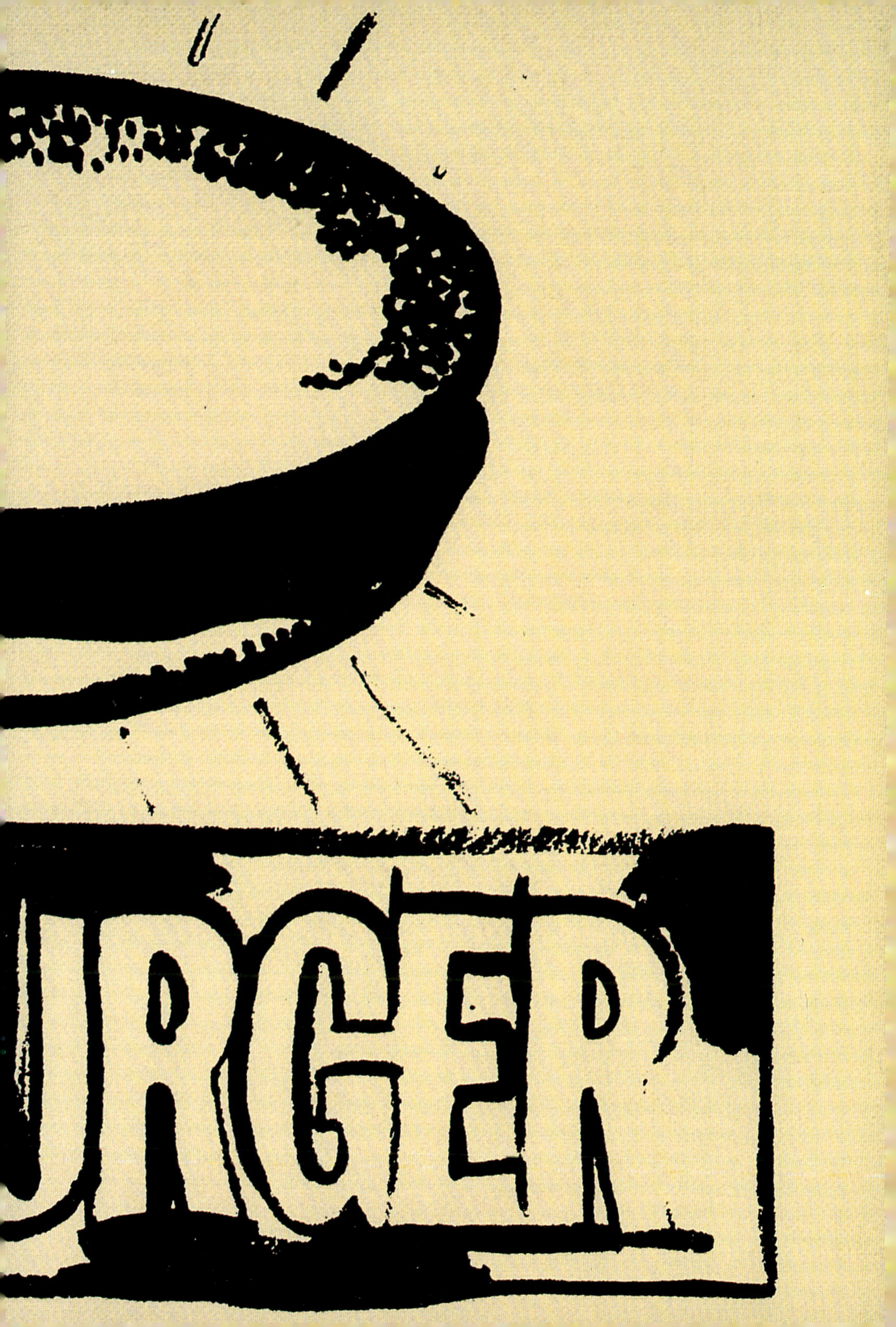
URGER

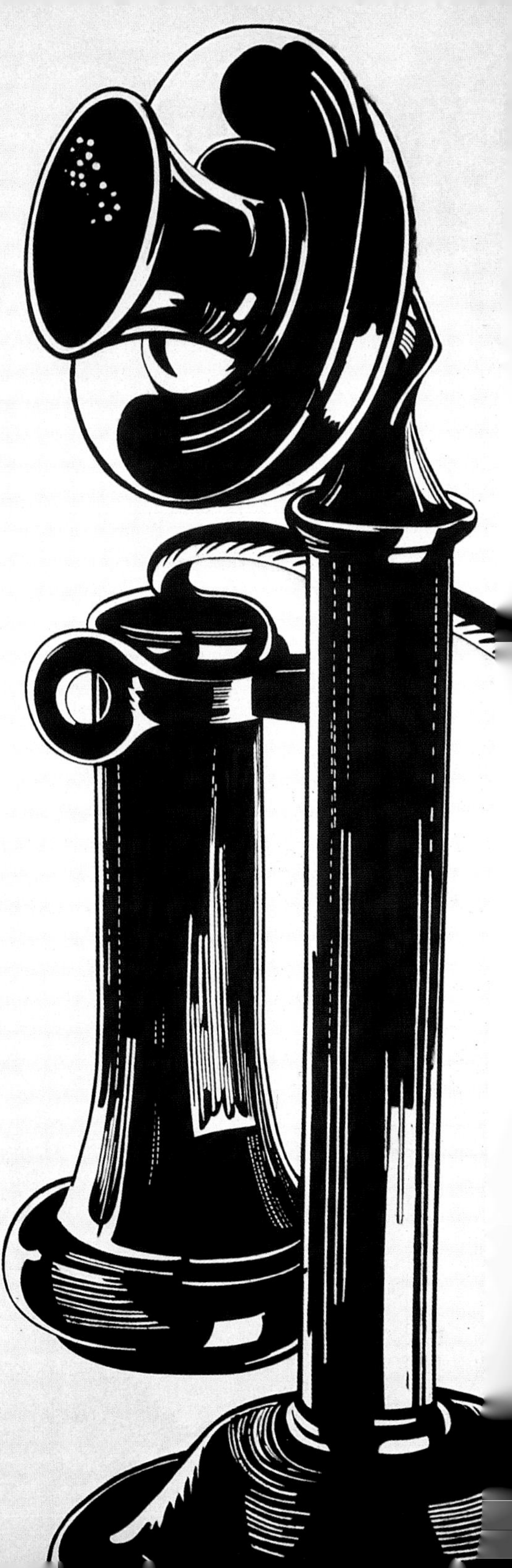

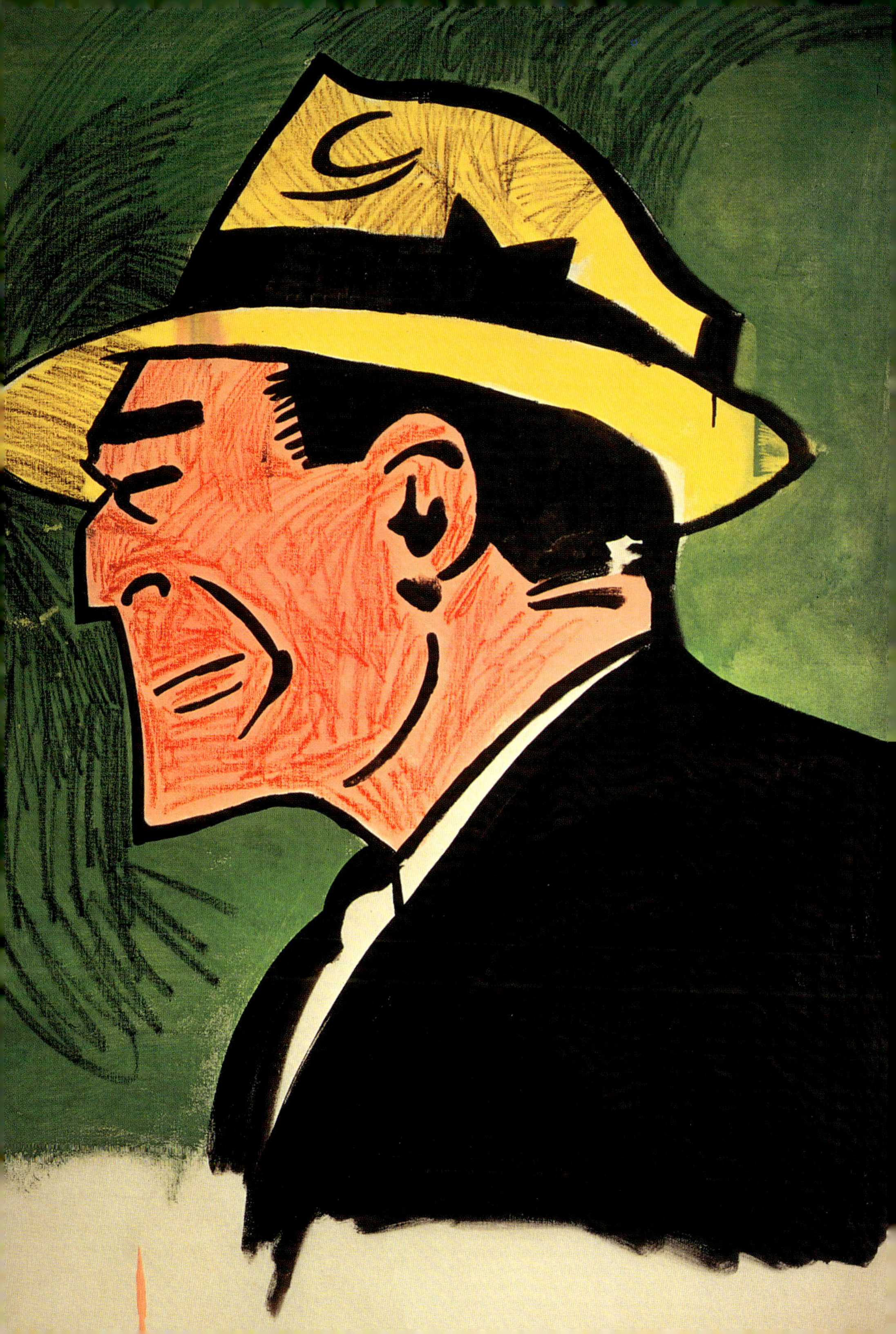

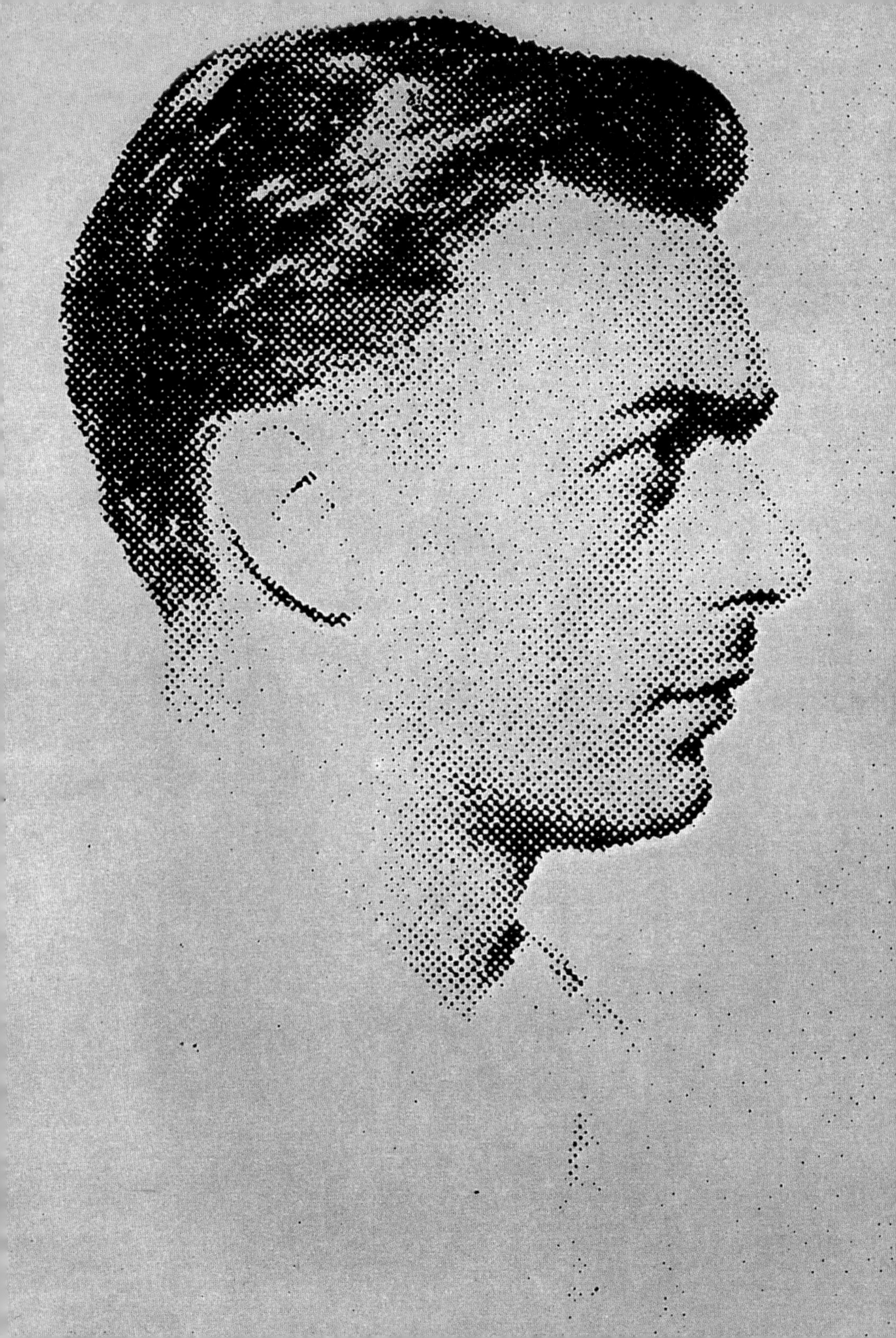

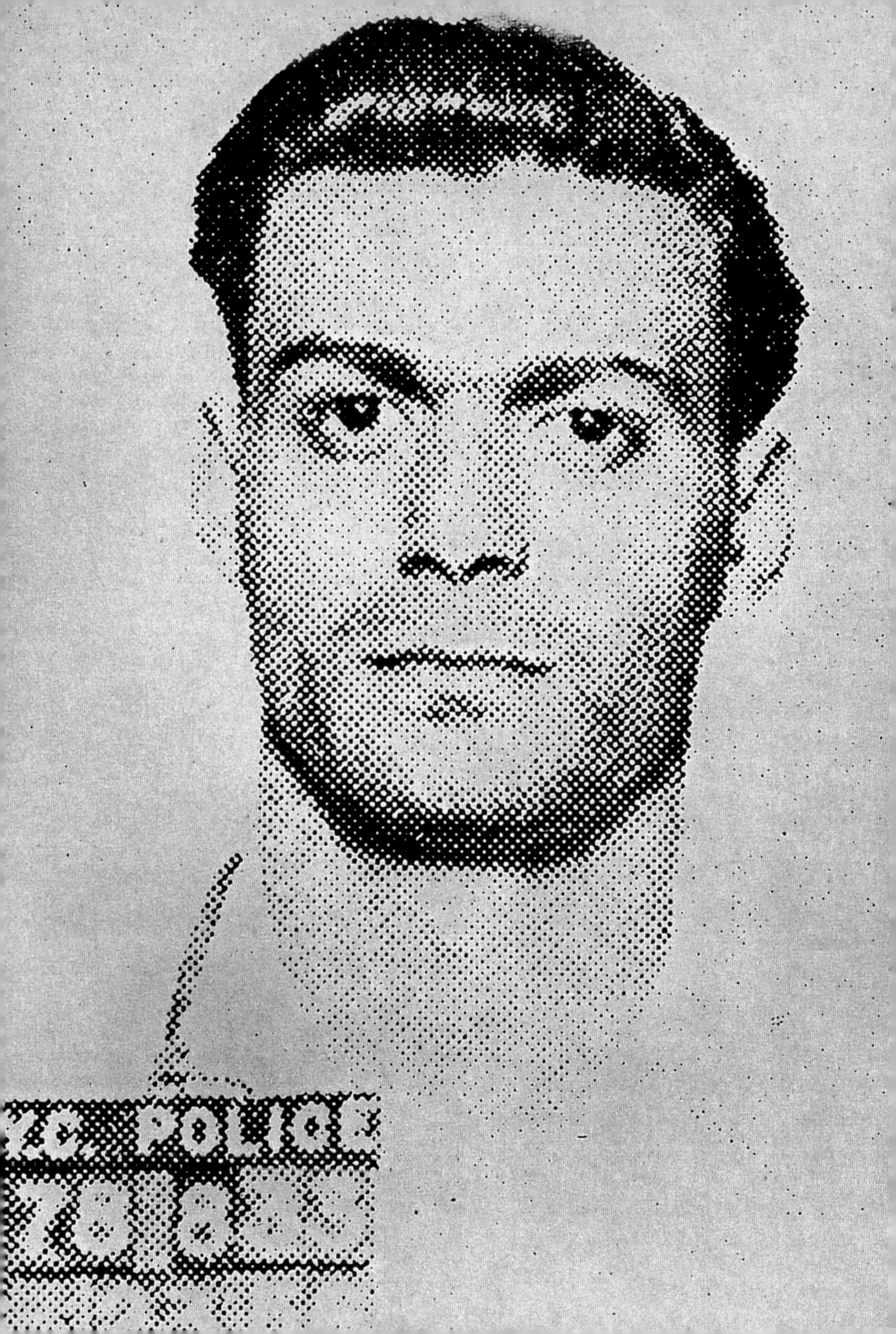

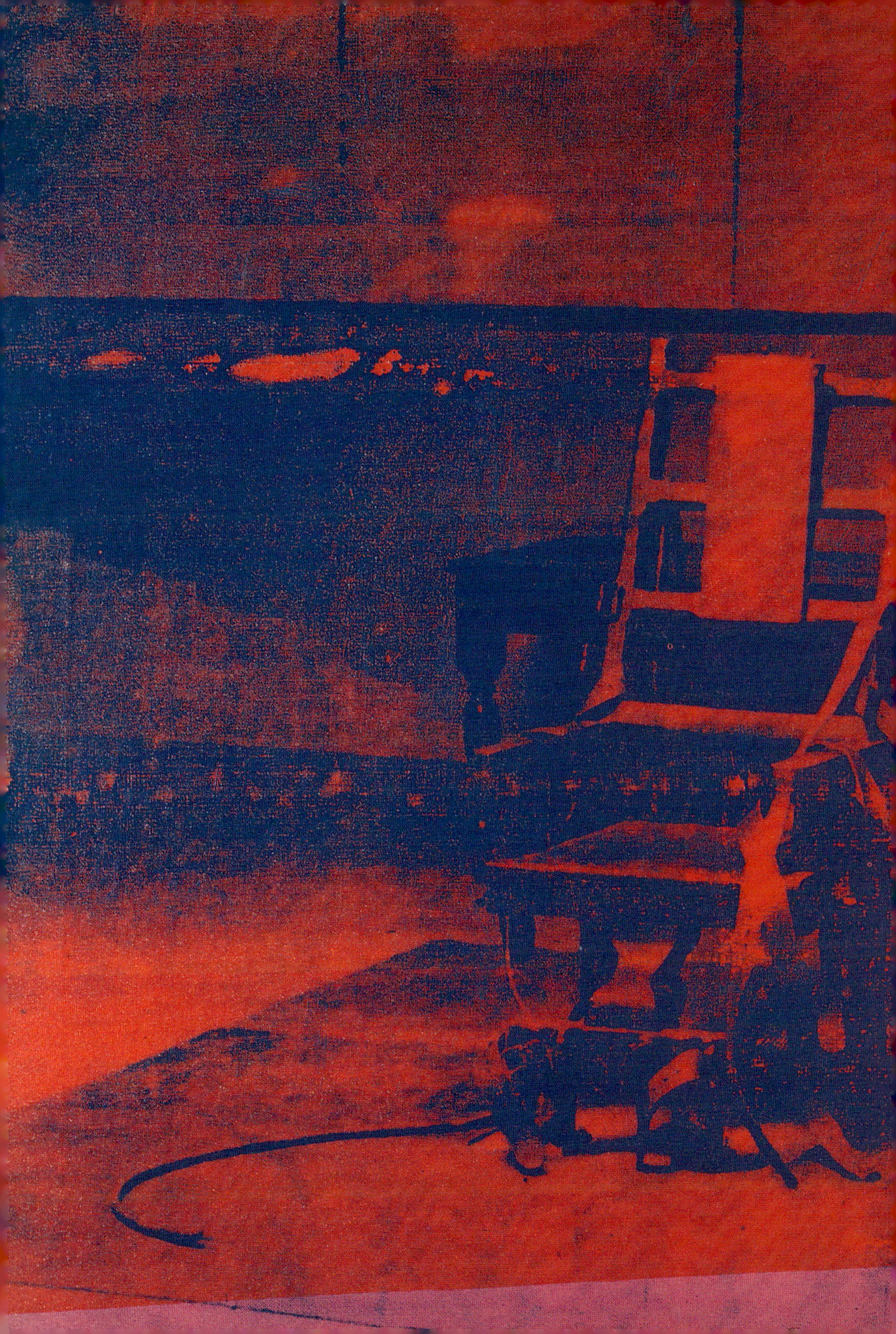

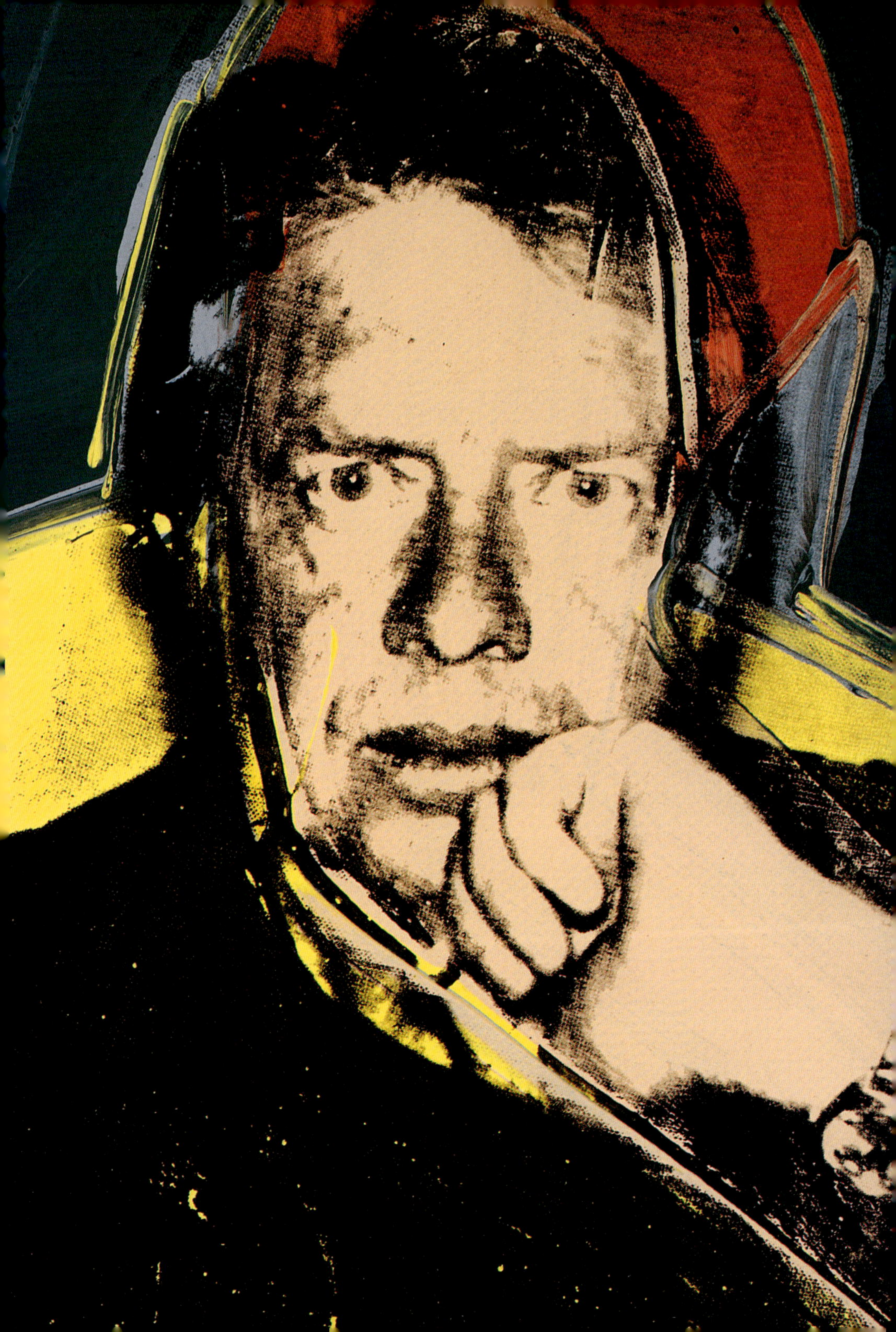

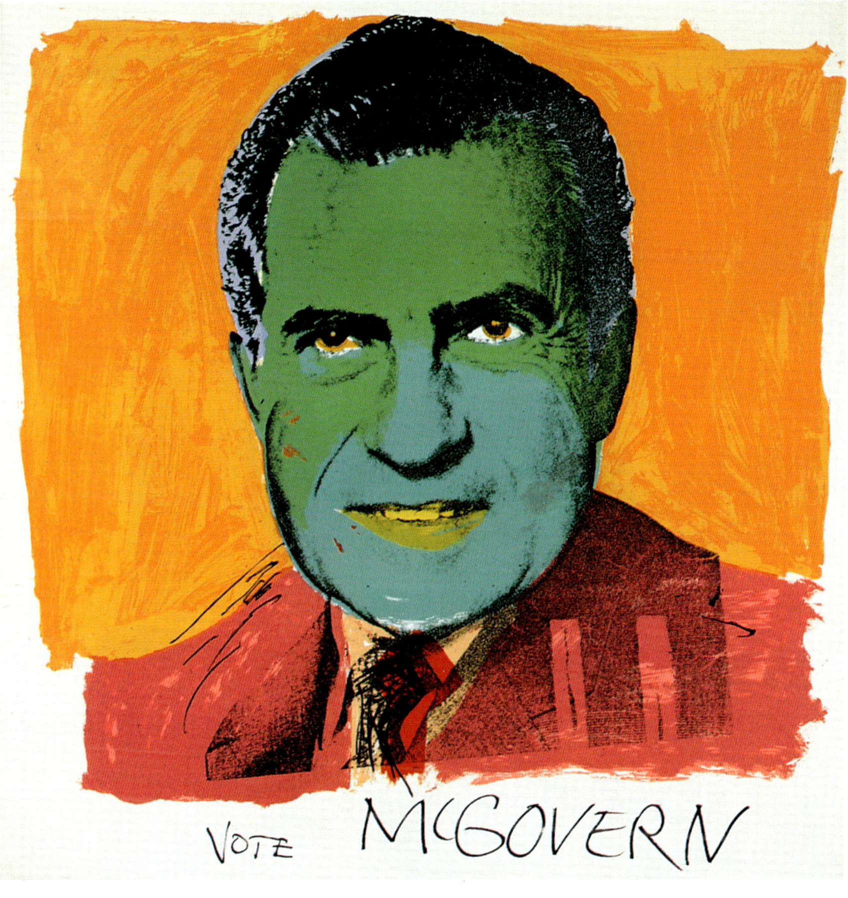
VOTE McGOVERN

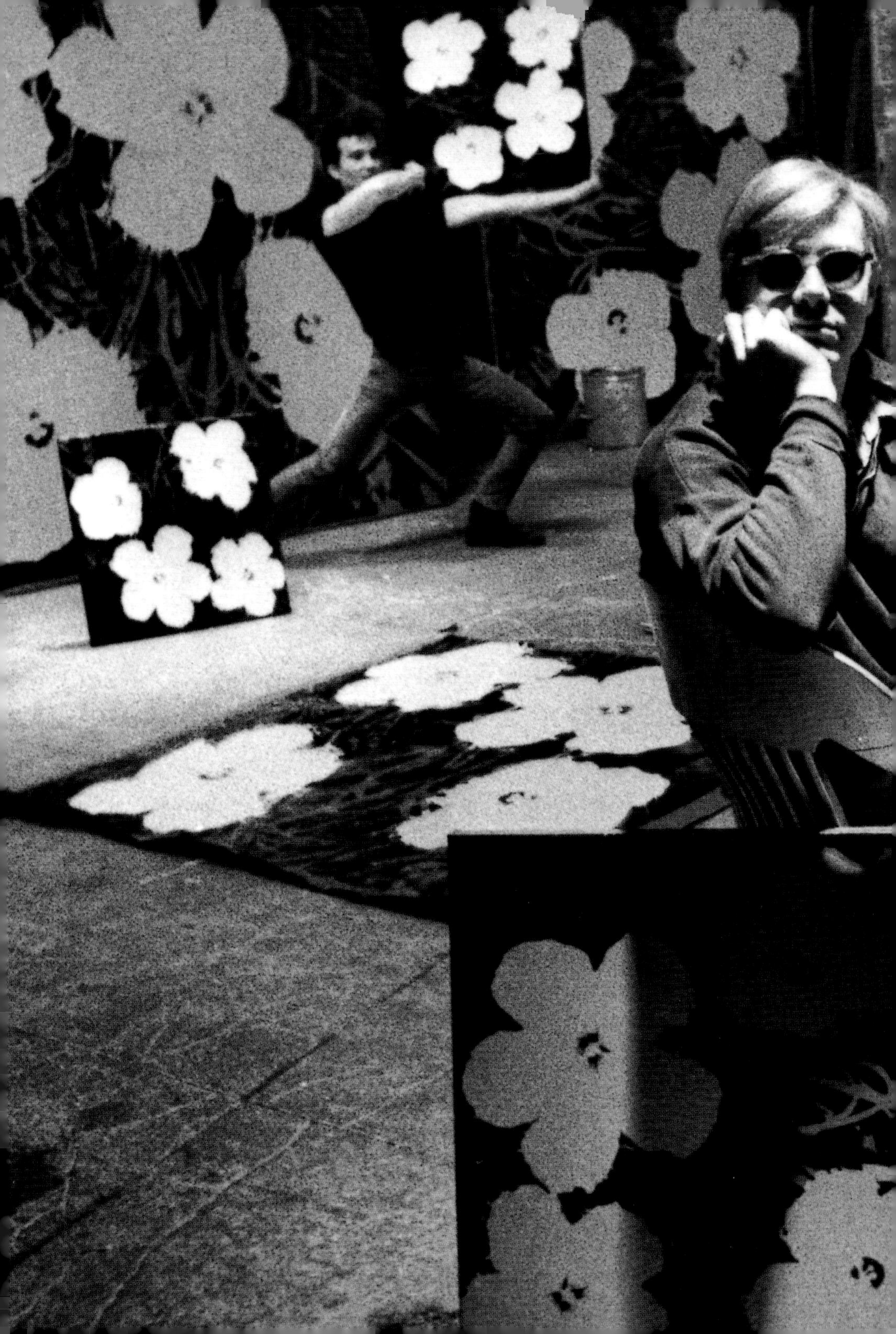

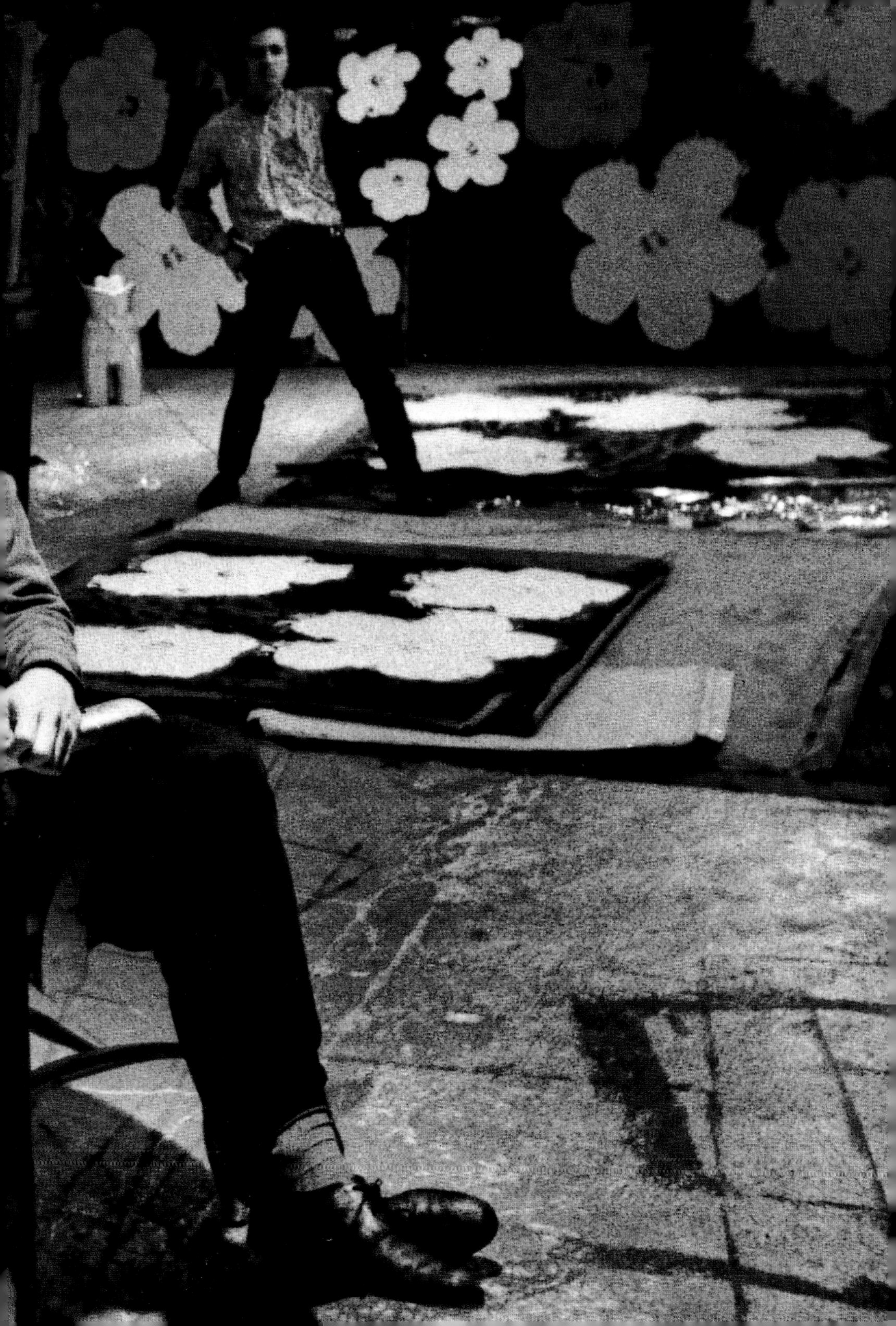

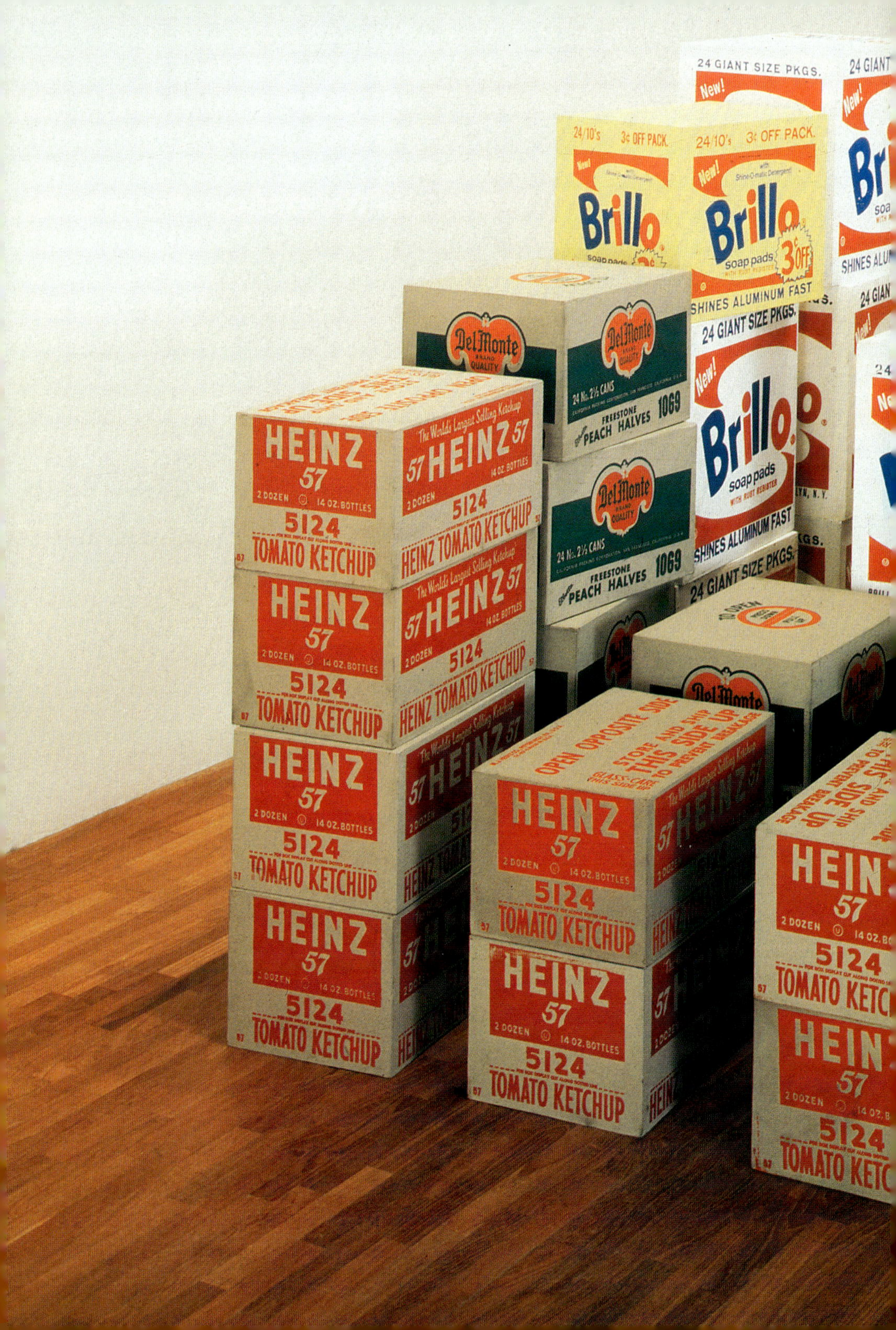
24 GIANT SIZE PKGS.
New!
Brillo
soap pads
SHINES ALUMINUM FAST
24/10's 3¢ OFF PACK.
3¢ OFF
Del Monte
QUALITY
24 No. 2½ CANS
FREESTONE
PEACH HALVES
1069
The World's Largest Selling Ketchup
HEINZ
57
2 DOZEN 14 OZ. BOTTLES
5124
TOMATO KETCHUP
HEINZ TOMATO KETCHUP
OPEN OPPOSITE SIDE
STORE AND SHIP
THIS SIDE UP

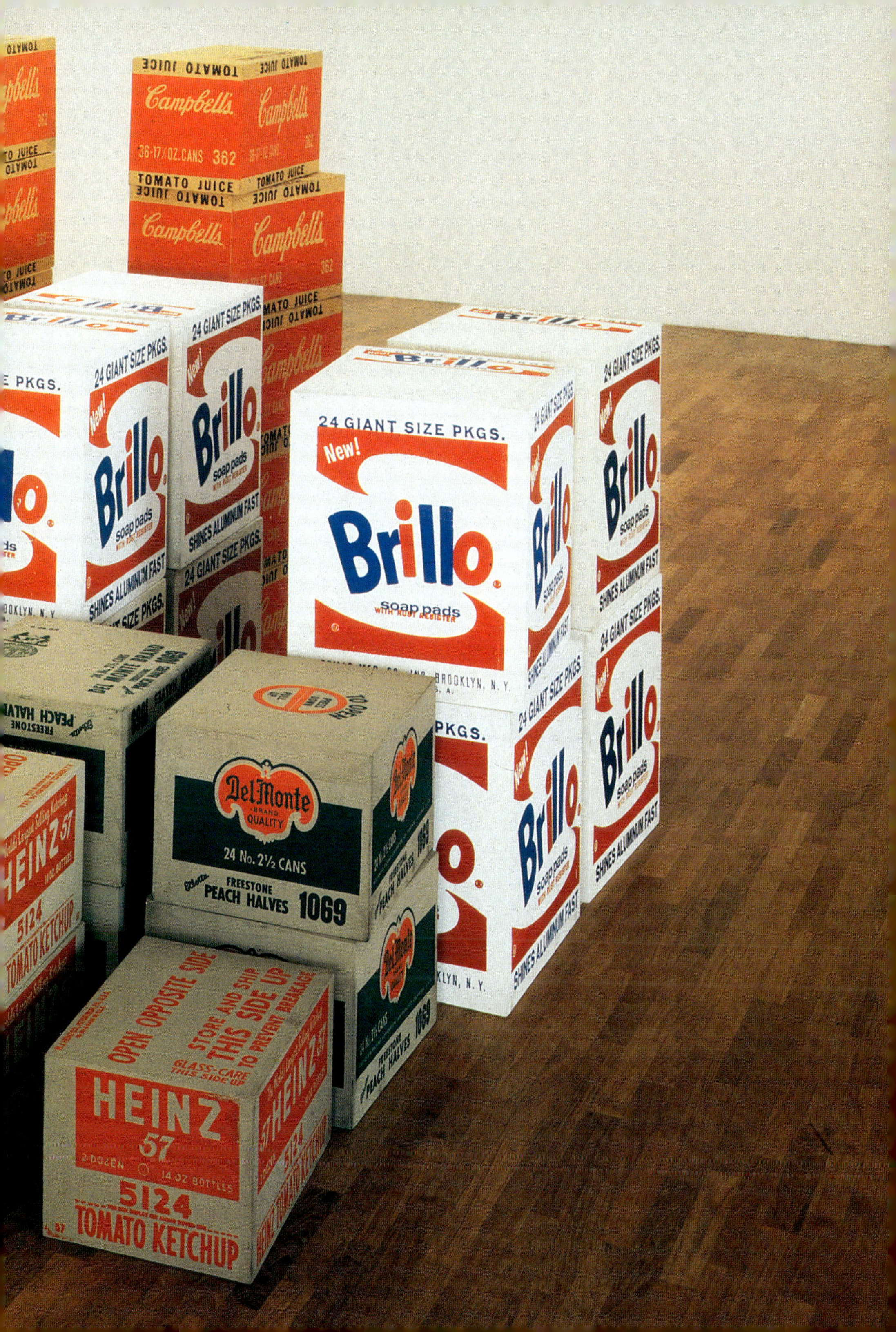
TOMATO JUICE
Campbell's
36-17 1/2 OZ. CANS 362
24 GIANT SIZE PKGS.
New!
Brillo
soap pads
SHINES ALUMINUM FAST
BROOKLYN, N. Y.
Del Monte
BRAND QUALITY
24 No. 2½ CANS
FREESTONE
PEACH HALVES 1069
TO OPEN
OPEN OPPOSITE SIDE
STORE AND SHIP THIS SIDE UP TO PREVENT BREAKAGE
GLASS-CARE THIS SIDE UP
HEINZ
57
2 DOZEN 14 OZ BOTTLES
5124
TOMATO KETCHUP

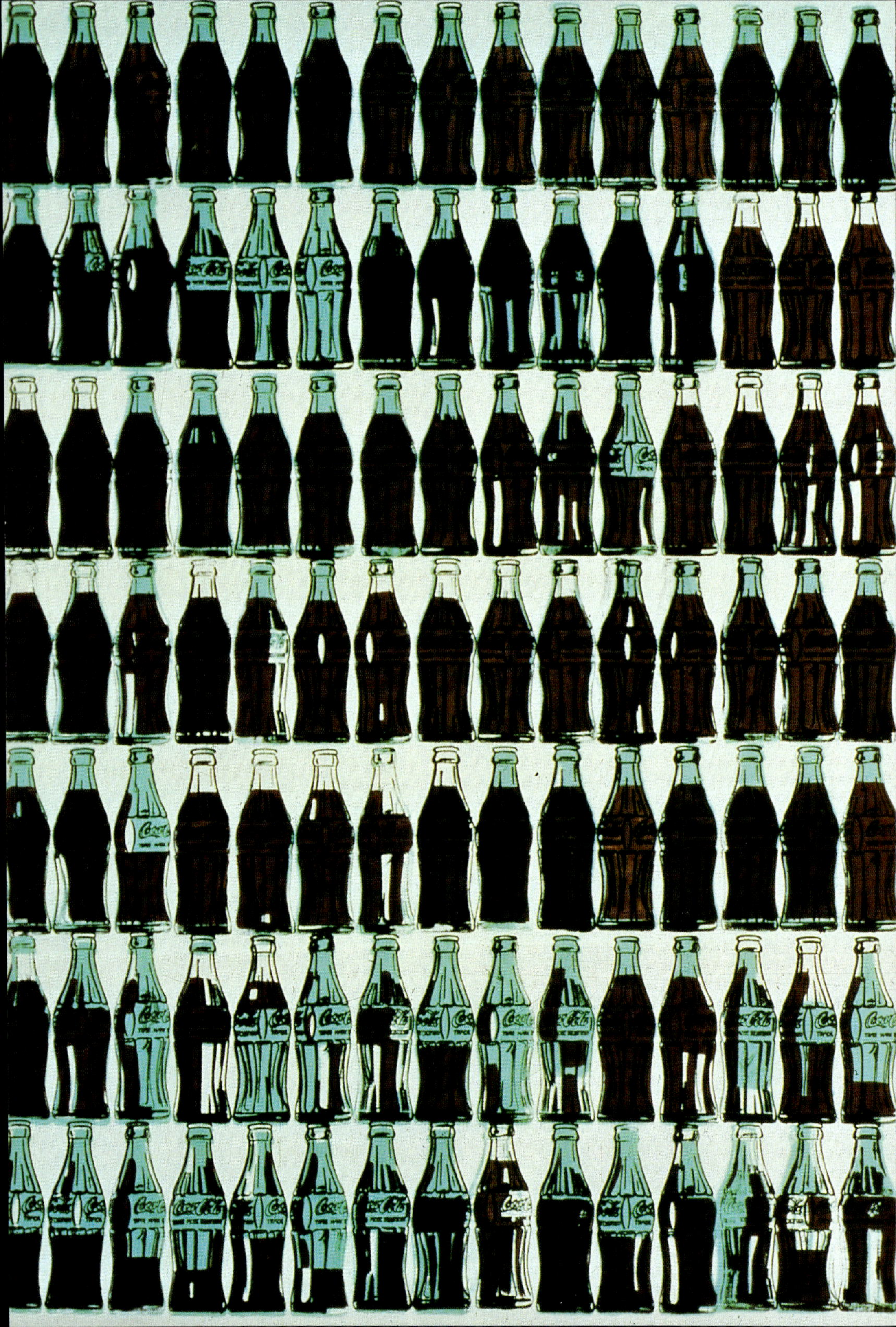
Coca-Cola

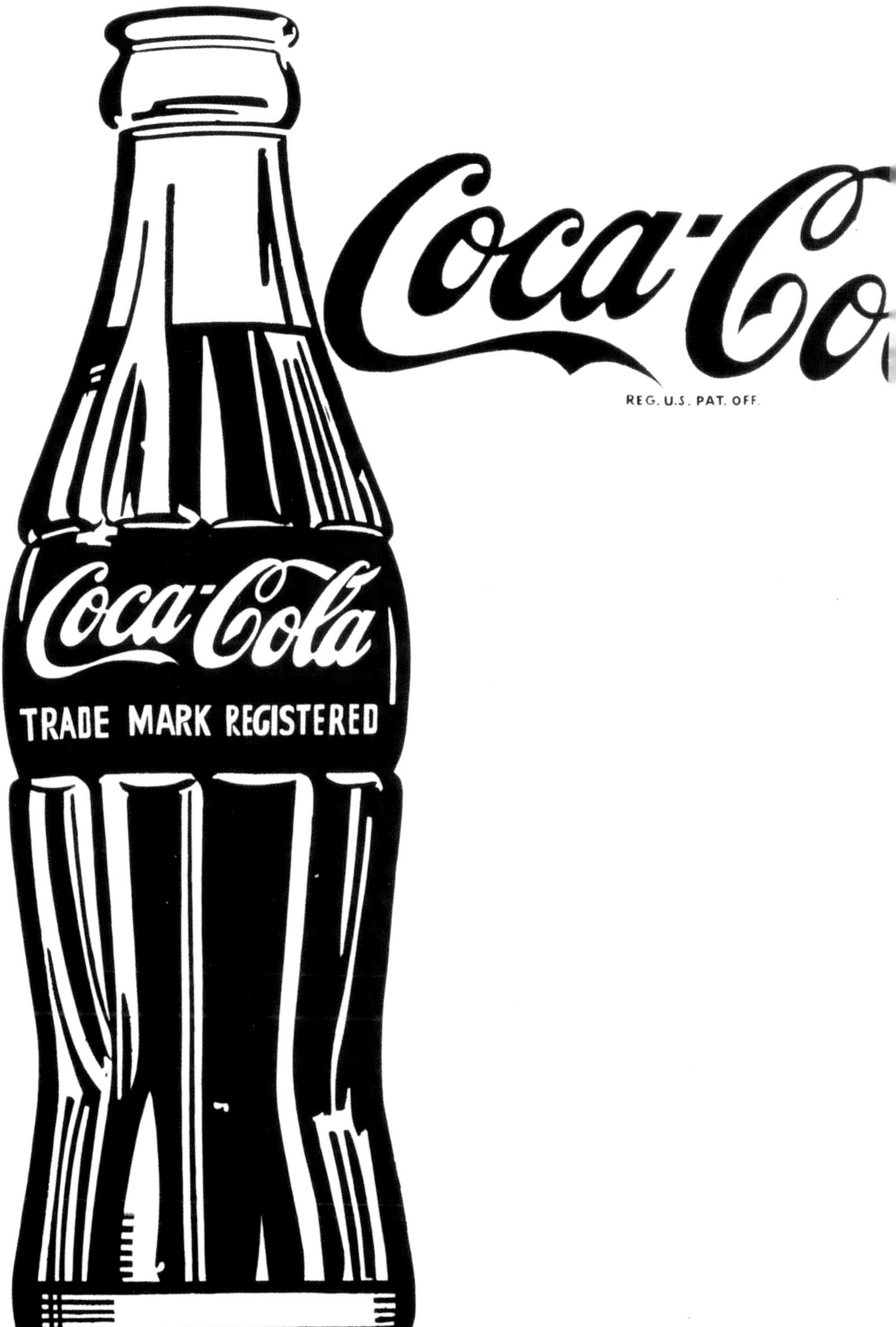
Coca-Cola
TRADE MARK REGISTERED
Coca-Co
REG. U.S. PAT. OFF.

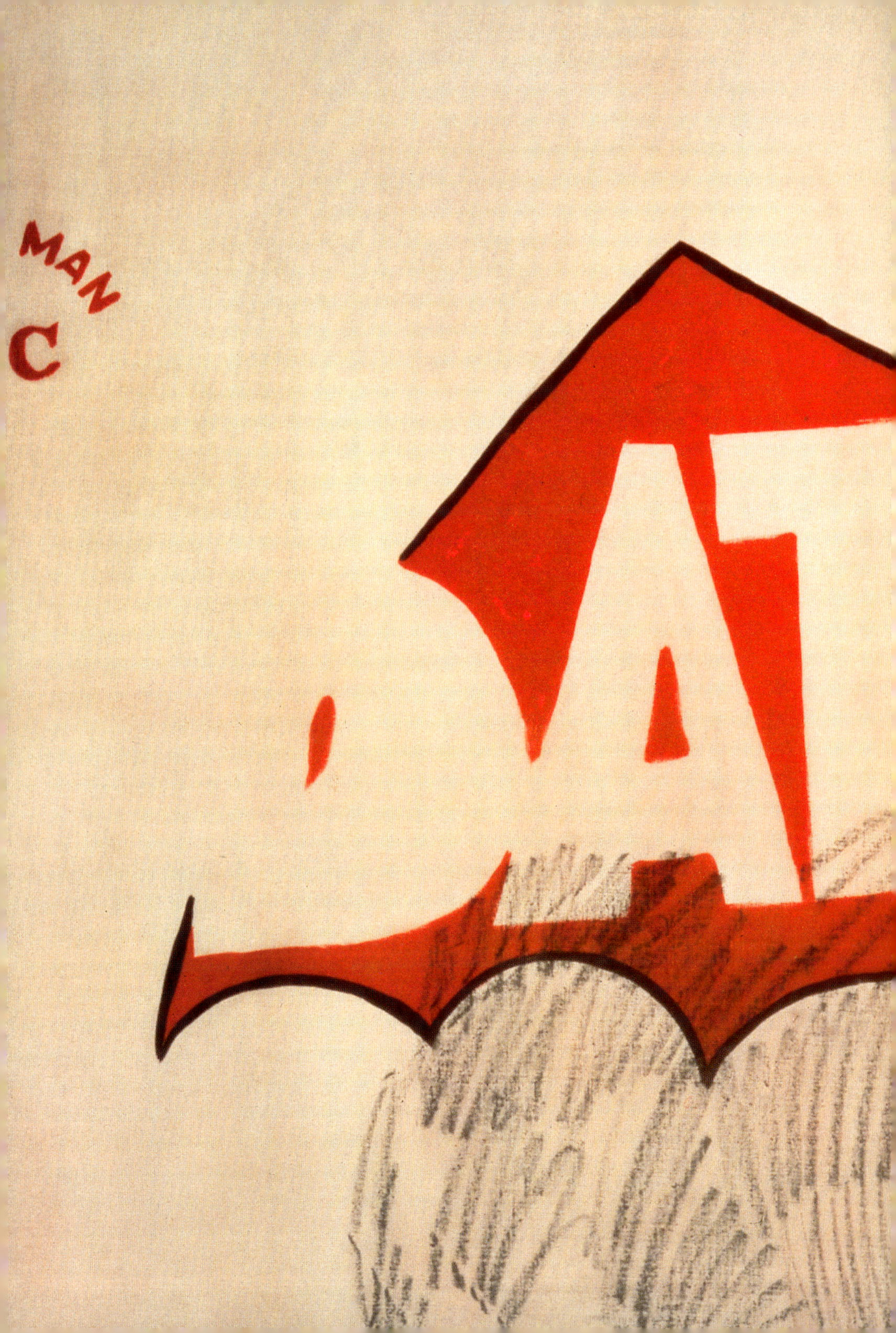
MAN
C

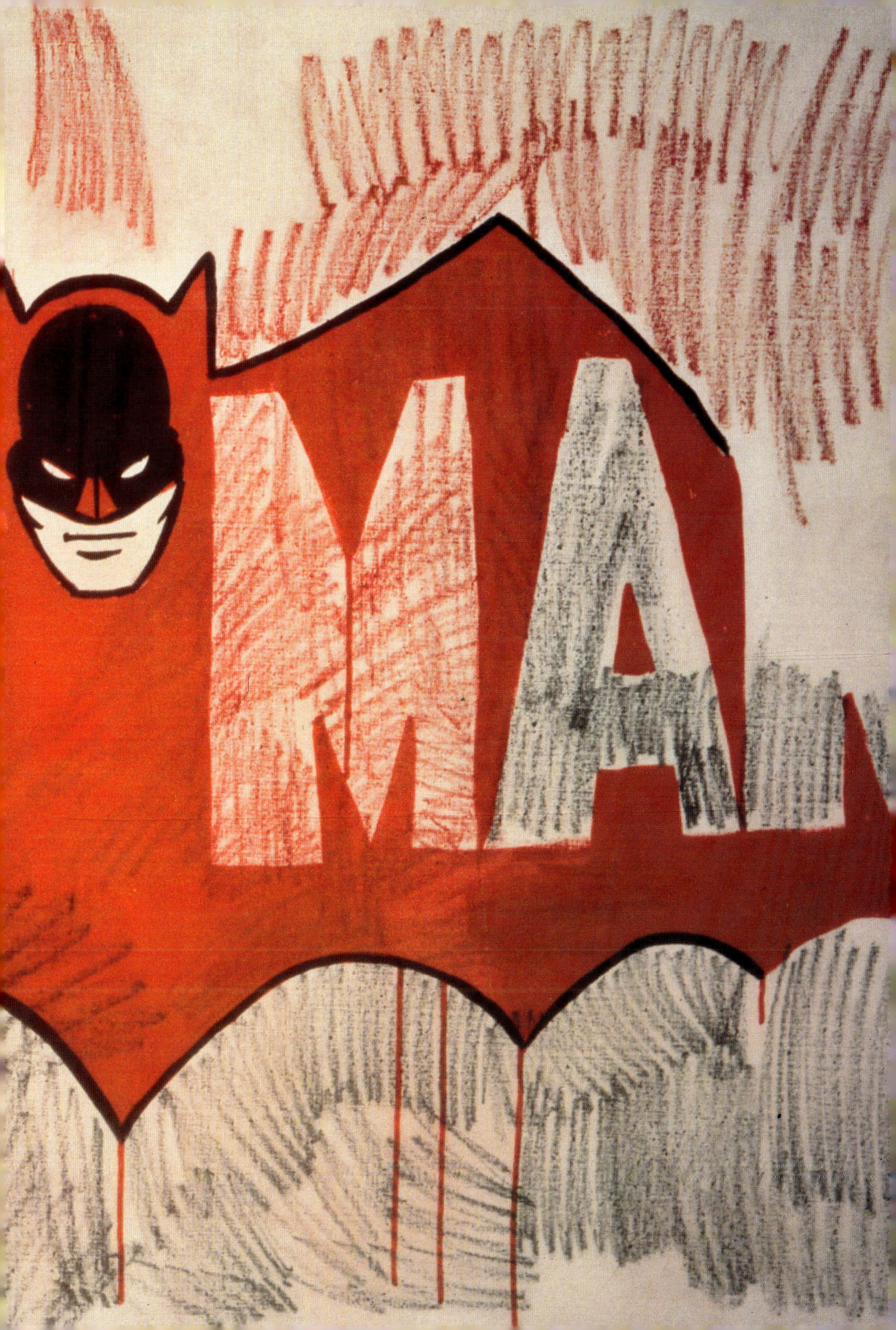
MA

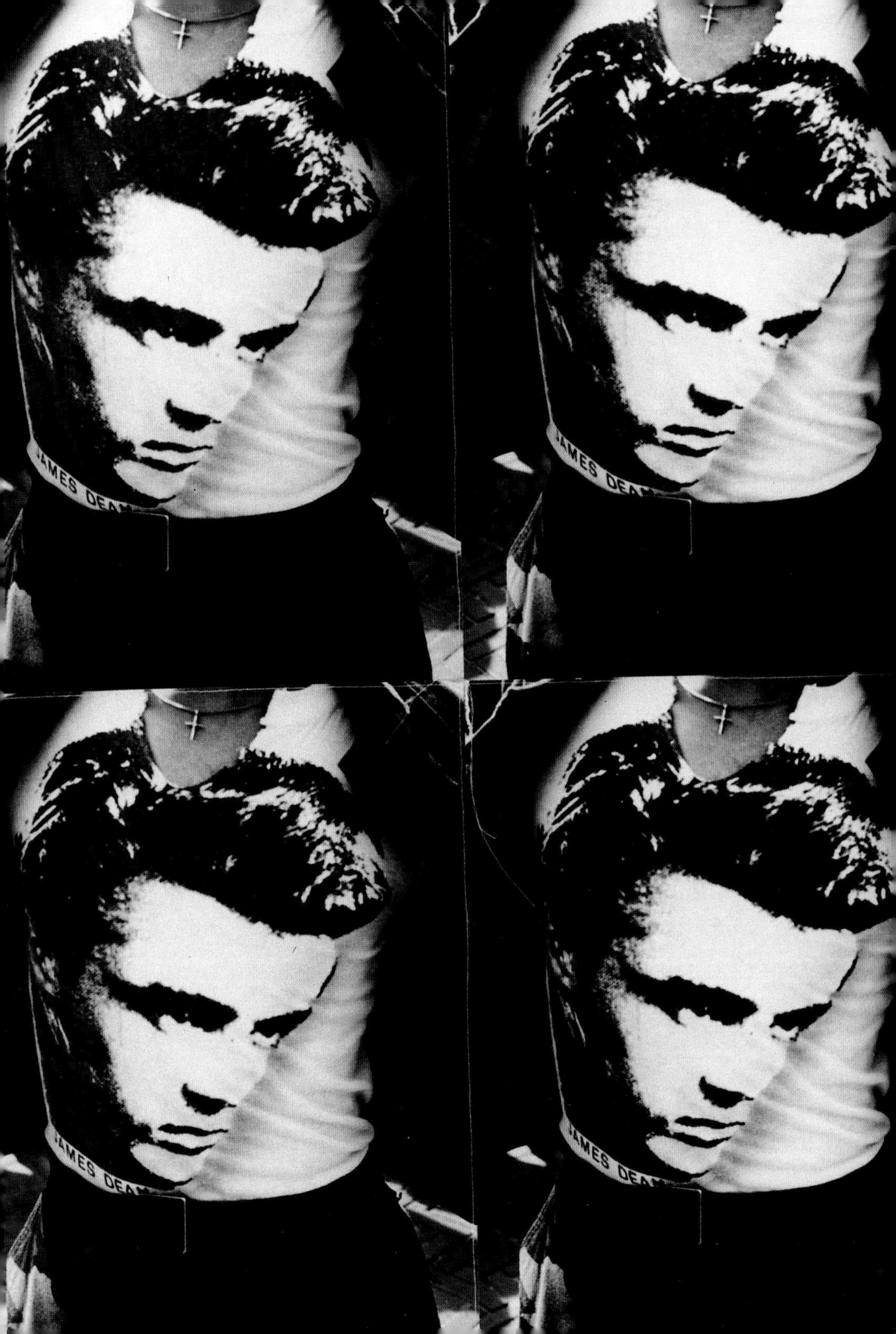
JAMES DEA
JAMES DEA
JAMES DEA
JAMES DEA

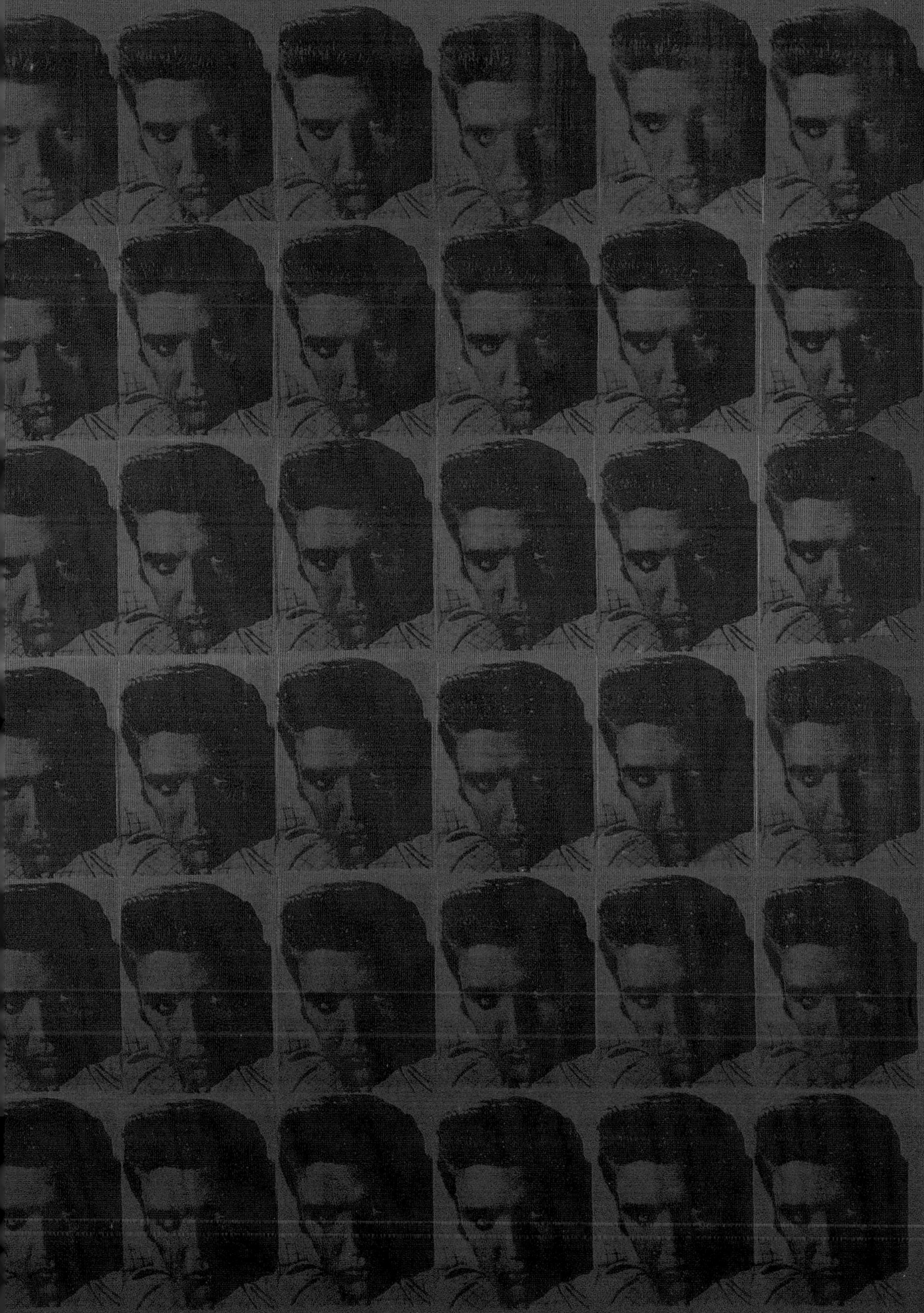

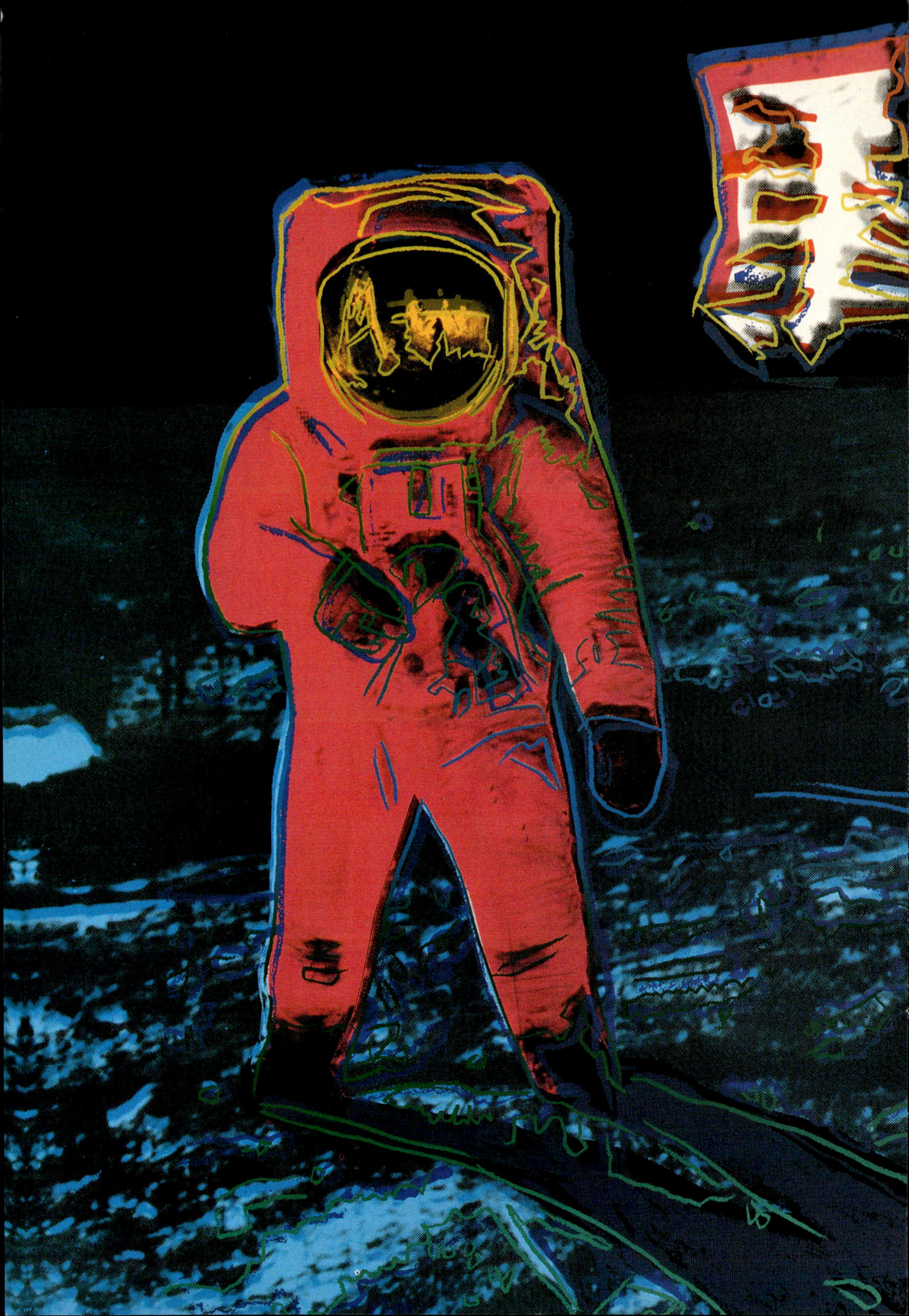

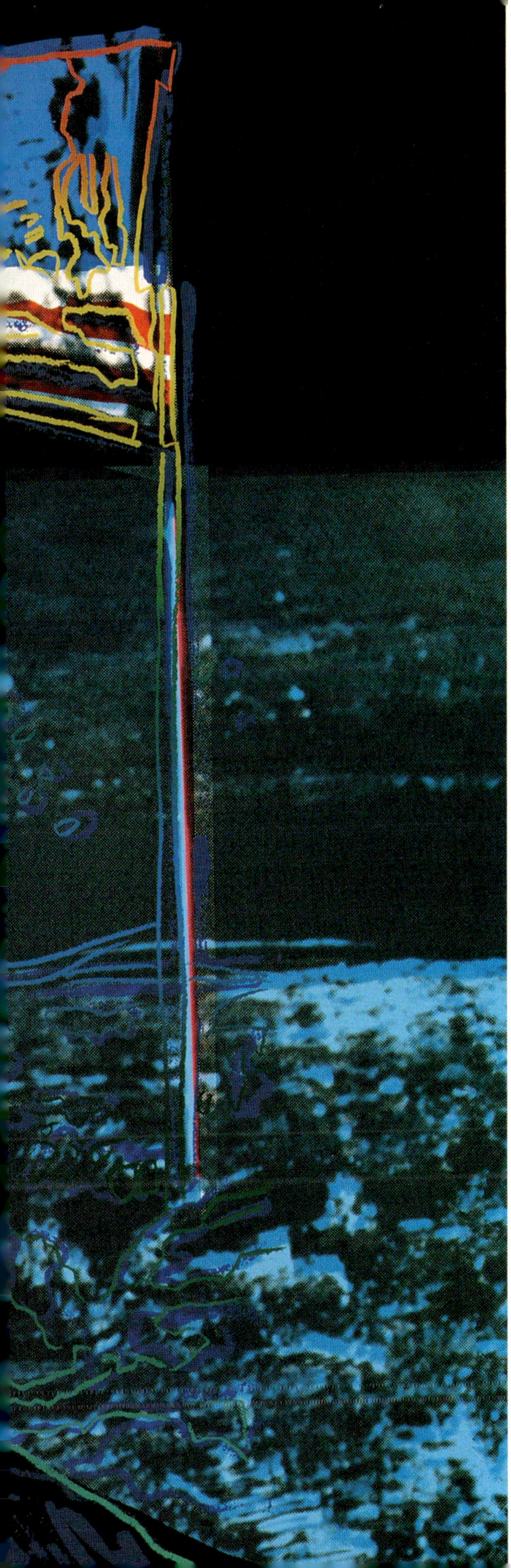

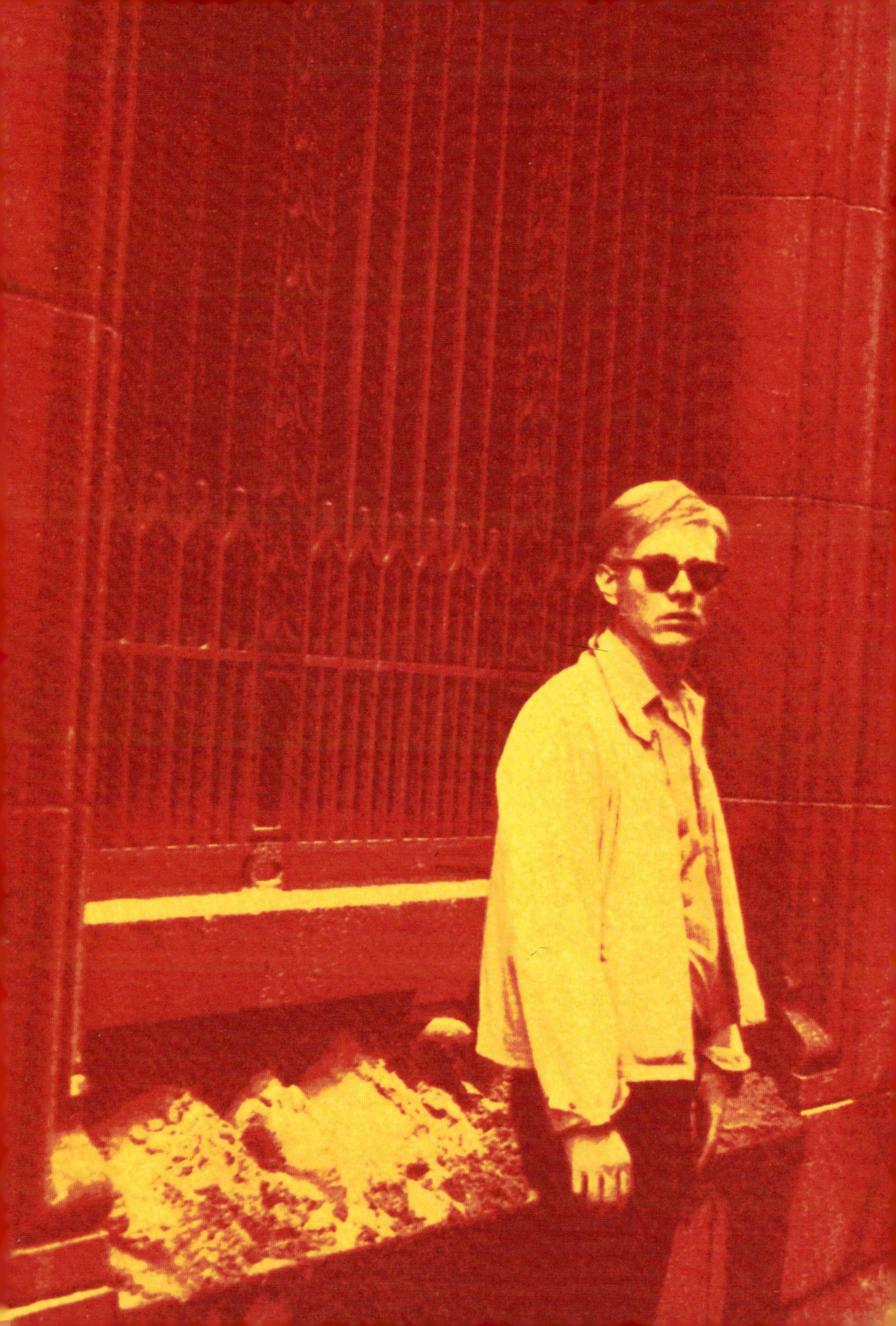

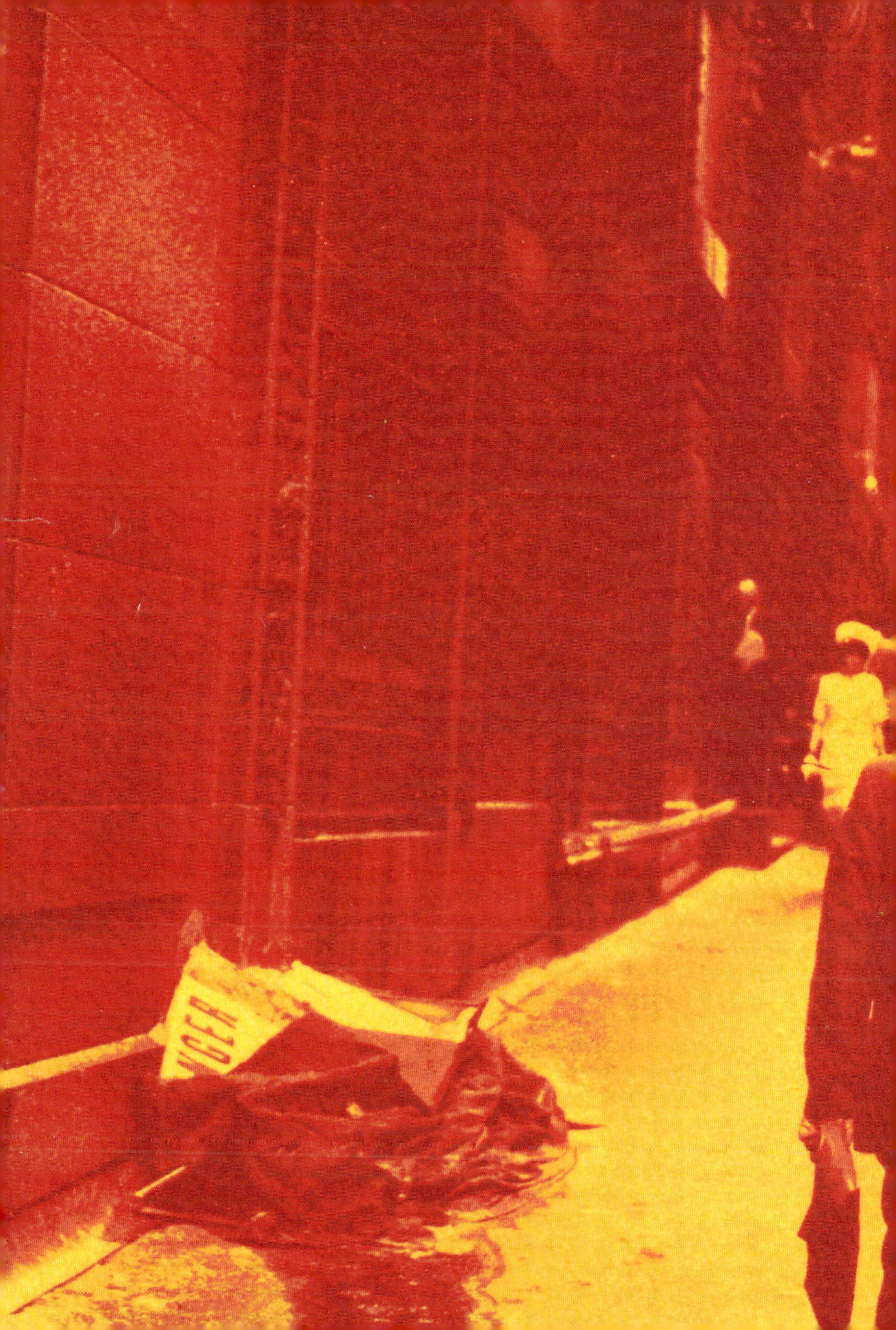

Chronology

1928	Born in Pittsburgh, the son of Czech immigrants.
1945–1949	Studies design, history of art and sociology at the Carnegie Institute of Technology, Pittsburgh. Graduates with a Bachelor of Arts degree. Meets Philip Pearlstein, with whom he shares a large studio.
1949	Moves to New York, where he and Pearlstein share an apartment. Beginning of his collaboration with the press working for *Glamour* magazine. Works for *Vogue* and *Harper's Bazaar*, produces window displays for Bonwit Teller and his first commercial drawings for the shoe designers I. Miller.
1952	First one-man exhibition at the Hugo Gallery, New York, showing his drawings illustrating stories by Truman Capote, and stage designs. Dyes his hair blond and moves with his mother and numerous cats to a house on Lexington Avenue.
1954	Makes a name for himself as an illustrator of women's fashion accessories, particularly shoes.
1956	Exhibition of the drawings for *Boy Book* at the Bodley Gallery, New York. Exhibition of *Golden Shoes* in Madison Avenue. Travels in Asia and Europe.
1960	First paintings drawing on comic strips and commercial images.
1962	Silkscreen prints on canvas (dollar bills, *Campbell's Soup*, *Marilyn Monroe*). Takes part in the group exhibition 'The New Realists' at the Sidney Janis Gallery, New York. Beginning of the 'disaster series': *White Car Crash*, *Suicide* and *Electric Chair*.
1963	Makes the films *Sleep* and *Empire*, each over six hours long.
1964	Exhibition of the *Flowers* series at the Galerie Sonnabend, Paris. *Thirteen Most Wanted Men*, produced for the New York State pavilion at the World Fair held in New York, has to be repainted for political reasons. First sculptures using collage of silkscreens of cardboard cartons.
1965	Exhibition at the Institute of Contemporary Art, Philadelphia. Makes the film *My Hustler*.

1966– Films with the Velvet Underground. Makes *Chelsea Girls*.

1968 Leo Castelli exhibits the *Cow Wallpapers* and the *Silver Pillows*.

1968 Exhibition at the Moderna Museet, Stockholm.
In July, he is shot and seriously wounded by Valerie Solanas, the founder and sole member of SCUM (Society for Cutting Up Men). Publication of the 'tape novel' *A*, which is in fact a transcription of telephone conversations at the 'factory'.

1969 First issue of the magazine *Interview*, of which he is co-editor.
Beginning of portrait commissions, including *Yves Saint Laurent* and *David Hockney*.

1970 Production of his first film *Flesh*.

1971 Exhibition at the Whitney Museum of American Art, New York.

1972 Exhibition at the Kunstmuseum, Basle.

1975 Publication of his book *The Philosophy of Andy Warhol (From A to B and Back Again)*.

1978 *Oxidations* and *Shadows* series.

1979 Exhibition at the Whitney Museum of American Art, New York.

1980 Becomes the executive producer of the cable TV station 'Andy Warhol's TV'.
Exhibition 'Joseph Beuys by Andy Warhol' at the Centre d'Art Contemporain, Geneva.
Exhibition of *Ten Portraits of Jews of the Twentieth Century* at the Lowe Art Museum, the University of Miami and the Jewish Museum, New York.
Publication of *POPism: the Warhol 60's* by Warhol and Pat Hackett.

1982 Takes part in 'Documenta 7' held in Kassel, Germany, with the *Oxidations* series and images of Nazi architecture. Exhibits at the Castelli Gallery, New York, and at the Fernando Vijande Gallery, Madrid.

1984 Beginning of collaboration with Jean-Michel Basquiat. The following year, they exhibit together at the Shafrazi Gallery, New York.

1986 Portrait of Lenin and self-portraits.

1987 Dies after undergoing surgery.

1989 *Shot Red Marilyn* sold at Christie's for $4,000,000
Retrospective at the Museum of Modern Art, New York.

Warhol's America

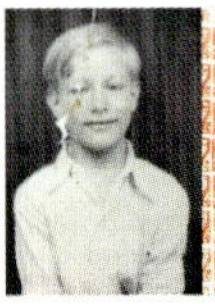
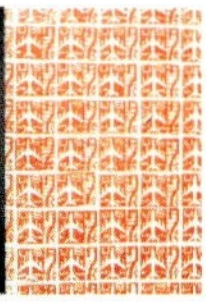

Pittsburgh blues. Taken in 1940, when Warhol was 12. 'When you're growing up in a small town ... You hate it and you know you'll have to leave' – fifty years later, John Cale and Lou Reed wrote these lyrics in homage to their dead friend. © The Archives of the Andy Warhol Museum, Pittsburgh; Founding Collection, Contribution The Andy Warhol Foundation for the Visual Arts, Inc. and ADAGP, 1997.
Red Airmail Stamps, 1962. Synthetic polymer paint on canvas. 50.8 x 40.6 cm. © The Andy Warhol Foundation for the Visual Arts, Inc. and ADAGP, 1997.

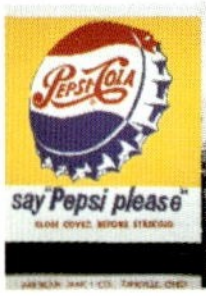

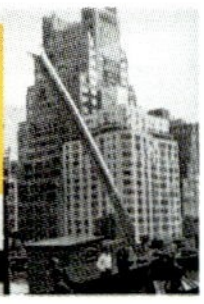

Close Cover Before Striking (Pepsi Cola), 1962. Synthetic polymer paint and sand paper on canvas. 1.82 x 1.35 m. © The Andy Warhol Foundation for the Visual Arts, Inc.
Earth, wind and fire. In 1965, influenced by Land Art and Ephemeral Art, Warhol and his followers prepare to release a helium-filled silver cloud into the New York sky from the roof of the 'factory'. © Billy Name.

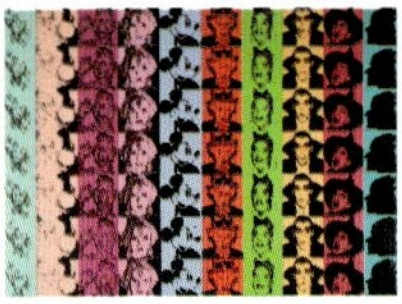

Myths, 1981. Synthetic polymer paint and silkscreen ink on canvas. 2.54 x 2.54 m. © The Andy Warhol Foundation for the Visual Arts, Inc. and ADAGP, 1997.

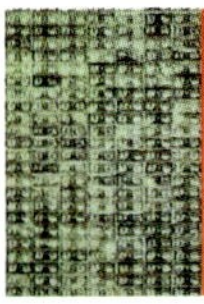
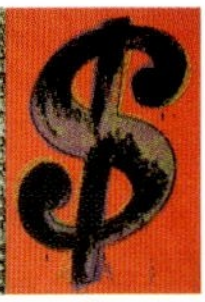

192 One Dollar Bills, 1962. © Sammlung Marx im Hamburger Bahnhof Museum für Gegenwart – Berlin and ADAGP, 1997.
Dollar Sign, c. 1981. Synthetic polymer paint and silkscreen ink on canvas. 2.28 x 1.78 m. © The Andy Warhol Foundation for the Visual Arts, Inc. and ADAGP, 1997.

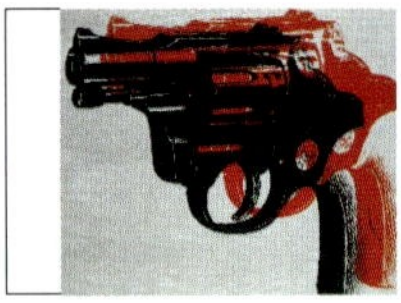

Gun, c. 1981–82. Synthetic polymer paint and silkscreen ink on canvas. 40.6 x 50.8 cm. © The Andy Warhol Foundation for the Visual Arts, Inc. and ADAGP, 1997.

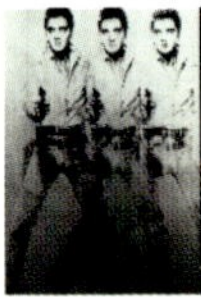
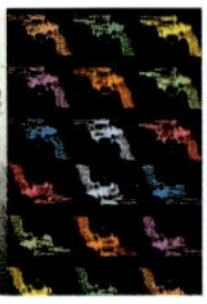

Triple Elvis, 1962. Silkscreen ink and aluminium paint on canvas. 2.08 x 1.52 m. © The Andy Warhol Foundation for the Visual Arts, Inc. and ADAGP, 1997.
Guns, c. 1982. Synthetic polymer paint and silkscreen ink on canvas. 1.32 x 1.77 m. © The Andy Warhol Foundation for the Visual Arts, Inc. and ADAGP, 1997.

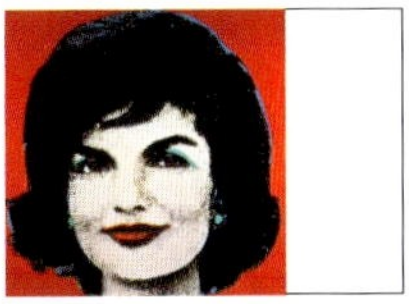

Jackie, 1963. Synthetic polymer paint and silkscreen ink on canvas. 1 x 1 m. © The Andy Warhol Foundation for the Visual Arts, Inc. and ADAGP, 1997.

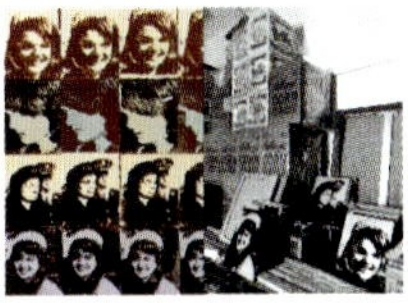

16 Jackies, 1964. Synthetic polymer paint and silkscreen ink on canvas. 2.03 x 1.62 m. © The Andy Warhol Foundation for the Visual Arts, Inc. and ADAGP, 1997.
Super market. A studied mixture of Warhol's works: Kellogg's Corn Flakes and Brillo pad cartons and different versions of *Jackie*. © Ugo Mulas Archives, Milan.

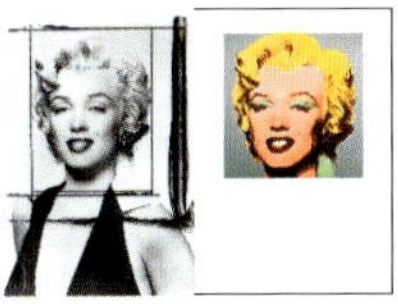

Marilyn in black and white, 1962. The photo that inspired Warhol's *Marilyn* paintings. An inscription at the top of the photo reads: 'Enlarge to 11 inches BM [between the marks]'. Ink on black-and-white photo. 25.4 x 20.3 cm. © The Archives of the Andy Warhol Museum, Pittsburgh; Founding Collection, Contribution The Andy Warhol Foundation for the Visual Arts, Inc. and ADAGP, 1997.
Marilyn, 1964. Synthetic polymer paint and silkscreen ink on canvas. 1 x 1 m. © The Andy Warhol Foundation for the Visual Arts, Inc. and ADAGP, 1997.

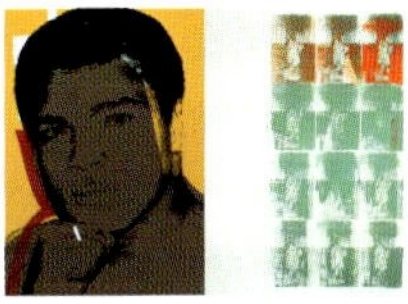

Muhammad Ali, 1978. Part of a portfolio of four silkscreen ink prints on Strathmore paper. 100 x 81.3 cm. © The Andy Warhol Foundation for the Visual Arts, Inc. and ADAGP, 1997.
Statue of Liberty, 1963. Synthetic polymer paint and silkscreen ink on canvas. 2 x 1.55 m. © The Andy Warhol Foundation for the Visual Arts, Inc. and ADAGP, 1997.

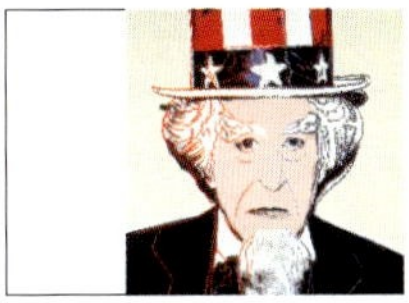

Myths: Uncle Sam, 1981. Part of a portfolio of 10 silkscreen ink prints on 'Lenox Museum' panel. 96.5 x 96.5 cm. © The Andy Warhol Foundation for the Visual Arts, Inc. and ADAGP, 1997.

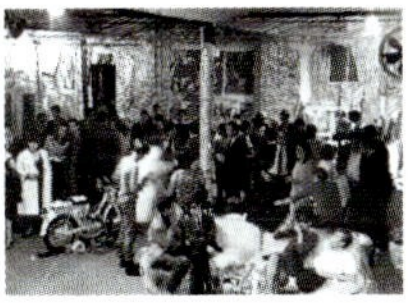

'Factory'. Typical everyday scene at the 'factory' in 1965. Open doors, silver walls, celebrities, alcohol, etc. On the sofa, Shirley Clarke and Steven Shore wearing sunglasses. In the background on the right, Andy Warhol seen in three-quarter view. © Fred W. McDarrah.

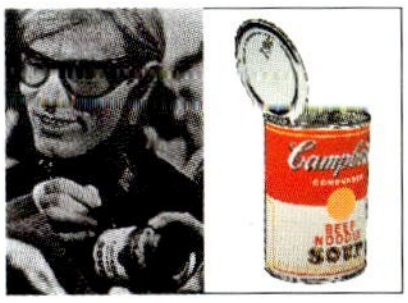

Yes I 'can'. Andy Warhol autographing a real Campbell's soup can. The directors of Campbell's were unhappy about this unauthorized 'ad'. On receiving a 'Warhol' as a leaving present, the boss of the Campbell's company nearly choked. © All rights reserved.
Big Campbell's Soup Can, 19 cents, 1962. Synthetic polymer paint. 1.83 x 1.38 m. © The Andy Warhol Foundation for the Visual Arts, Inc. and ADAGP, 1997.

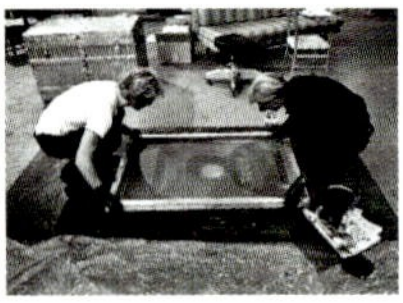

Copyright and wrong. Andy Warhol and Malanga in the process of silkscreening a Campbell's soup can. Mistakes in wedging and marks conferred on works produced in series the uniqueness of an original. © Ugo Mulas Archives, Milan.

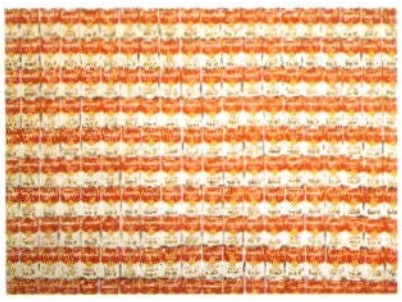

200 Campbell's Soup Cans, 1962. Synthetic polymer paint on canvas. 1.83 x 2.54 m. Collection John and Kimiko Powers. © The Andy Warhol Foundation for the Visual Arts, Inc. and ADAGP, 1997.

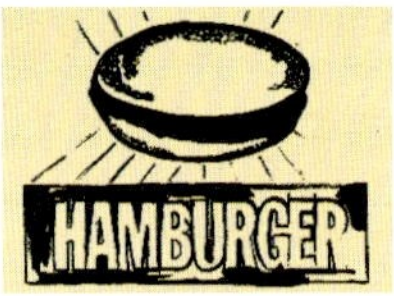

Hamburger (detail), *c.* 1985–86. Synthetic polymer paint and silkscreen ink on canvas. 25.4 x 30.4 cm. © The Andy Warhol Foundation for the Visual Arts, Inc. and ADAGP, 1997.

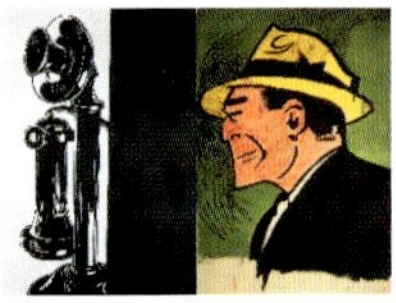

Telephone, 1961. Synthetic polymer paint and silkscreen ink on canvas. 2.54 x 1.83 m. © The Andy Warhol Foundation for the Visual Arts, Inc. and ADAGP, 1997.
Dick Tracy, 1960. Casein and crayon on canvas. 1.22 x 0.86 m. © The Andy Warhol Foundation for the Visual Arts, Inc. and ADAGP, 1997.

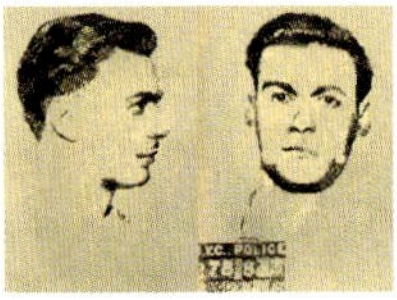

Most Wanted Men No. 10, 1964. Silkscreen ink on plaster and canvas. 1.22 x 1 m. © Städtisches Museum Abteiburg, Mönchengladbach and ADAGP, 1997.

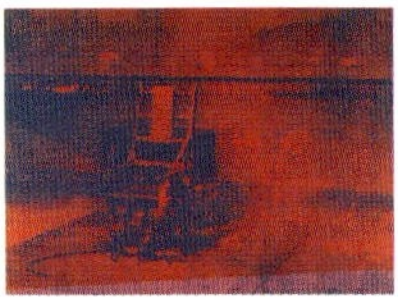

Electric Chair (red), 1966. Synthetic polymer paint and silkscreen ink on canvas. 1.37 x 1.85 m. Photo Philippe Migeat © Georges Pompidou Centre, Paris and ADAGP, 1997.

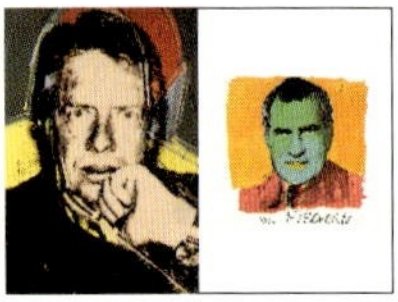

Jimmy Carter, 1976. Synthetic polymer paint and silkscreen ink on canvas. 10.1 x 27.9 cm. © The Andy Warhol Foundation for the Visual Arts, Inc. and ADAGP, 1997.
Vote McGovern, 1972. Silkscreen ink on Arches paper. 1.06 x 1.06 m. © The Andy Warhol Foundation for the Visual Arts, Inc.

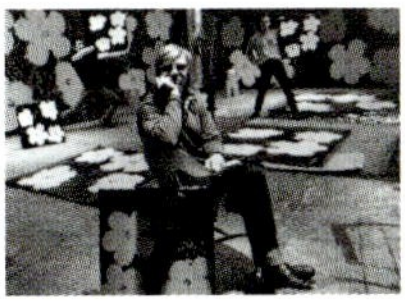

Workshop. During his 'flower' period, Andy Warhol allowed anyone who happened to be passing by the 'factory' to lend a hand. About 900 canvases were mass produced. © Ugo Mulas Archives, Milan.

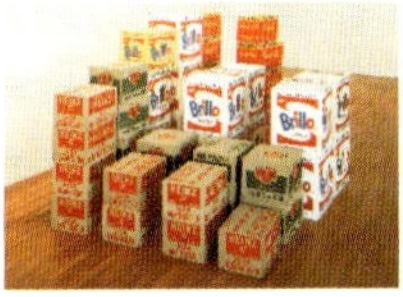

Various Box Sculptures, 1964. Silkscreen ink on wood. Various sizes. © The Andy Warhol Foundation for the Visual Arts, Inc. and ADAGP, 1997.

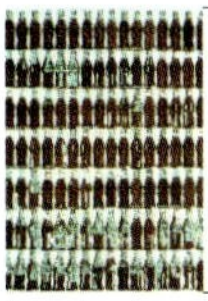
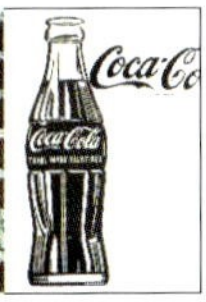

210 Coca-Cola Bottles, 1962. Synthetic polymer paint and silkscreen ink on canvas. 2.09 x 2.74 m. © The Andy Warhol Foundation for the Visual Arts, Inc. and ADAGP, 1997.
Large Coca-Cola, 1962. Synthetic polymer paint on canvas. 2.08 x 1.44 m. © The Andy Warhol Foundation for the Visual Arts, Inc. and ADAGP, 1997.

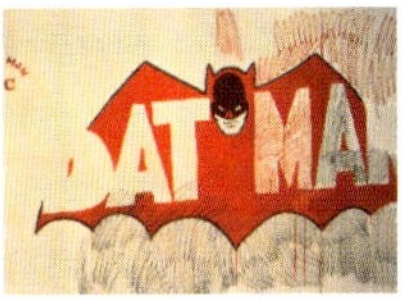

Batman, 1960. Synthetic polymer paint and crayon on canvas. 0.76 x 1 m. © The Andy Warhol Foundation for the Visual Arts, Inc. and ADAGP, 1997.

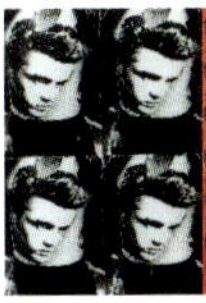

Untitled (James Dean T-Shirt), 1976–86. Four sewn gelatin-bromide prints. 71 x 56 cm. © The Andy Warhol Foundation for the Visual Arts, Inc. and ADAGP, 1997.
Red Elvis, 1962. Synthetic polymer paint and silkscreen ink on canvas. 1.75 x 1.32 m. © The Andy Warhol Foundation for the Visual Arts, Inc. and ADAGP, 1997.

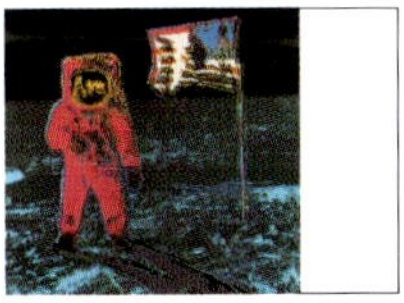

Moonwalk. Part of a portfolio of two silkscreen ink prints (special edition of 150 copies). 96 x 96 cm. Photo: D. James Dee. © Courtesy Ronald Feldman Fine Arts, New York and ADAGP, 1997.

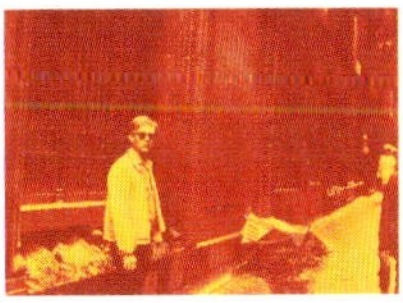

Play boy. Andy Warhol about 1965–66. During the rock explosion, Andy stuck to the 'mod', vaguely upper-class dandy look. © Billy Name.

The publishers wish to thank Billy Name, Fred W. McDarrah, Antonia Mulas, Camela Mulas and Valentina Mulas for their invaluable assistance. Thanks are due also to Nicole Chamson (ADAGP), Didier Schulman (Musée National d'Art Moderne), Beth Savage and Martin Cribbs (Andy Warhol Foundation for the Visual Arts), Mattew Wrbican (Andy Warhol Museum), Valentina Balzarotti Barbieri (Agenzia Letteraria Internazionale) and Hannelore Kersting (Städtisches Museum Abteiberg, Mönchengladbach).